Notes on Beelzebub's Tales

Volume 1: The Arousing of Thought

Compiled and Edited

by

Robin Bloor

KARNAK PRESS

Notes on Beelzebub's Tales

—

Volume 1: The Arousing of Thought

ISBN: 978-1-957278-17-9

Printed in the United States of America

KARNAK PRESS
Austin, Texas

DEDICATION

To G. Gurdjieff

And to his editors:

Alfred Richard Orage, Louise March
and
Jean De Salzmann

Notes on Beelzebub's Tales

"The preface is to the book what the overture is to an opera. Though frankly I did not and you probably will not understand this at all, yet you cannot afford to miss it."

~ Alfred Richard Orage

Notes on Beelzebub's Tales

Contents

The Arousing of Thought 9-15   71

Contents

The Arousing of Thought 22-28 147

Contents

Author's Biographical Notes

Acknowledgements

Foreword

This book, the first in what will become a sequence of volumes, is a detailed commentary on Gurdjieff's First Series, *The Tales*. The commentary comprises the assembled thoughts and ideas of four separate Tales Study Groups in which the author participated. All except the most recent one have been completed, from beginning to end.

The most recent one began in October 2025 and it will most likely continue for three more years, completing some time in 2029. For anyone who is interested, it is still possible to join and participate in this Tales Study Group.

If you wish to do so: you can register on this web page:

https://tofathomthegist.com/mem-tsg-sign-up-and-registration/

Or

Send an inquiry to: rbloor@littlecrowpress.com.

This book and those that follow focus on the series of readings that were the topic of specific study meetings. This first book of commentaries covers all the preface pages of *The Tales* and its first chapter, *The Arousing of Thought*. It comprises eight separate readings, the commentary on which form the eight chapters of this book. The next book will focus on ten or so subsequent readings

The individual commentary notes vary in length. Some may be just a sentence or two, providing simple context, the etymology of a word or phrase, while others may go into significant depth and cover several pages.

NOTES ON BEELZEBUB'S TALES

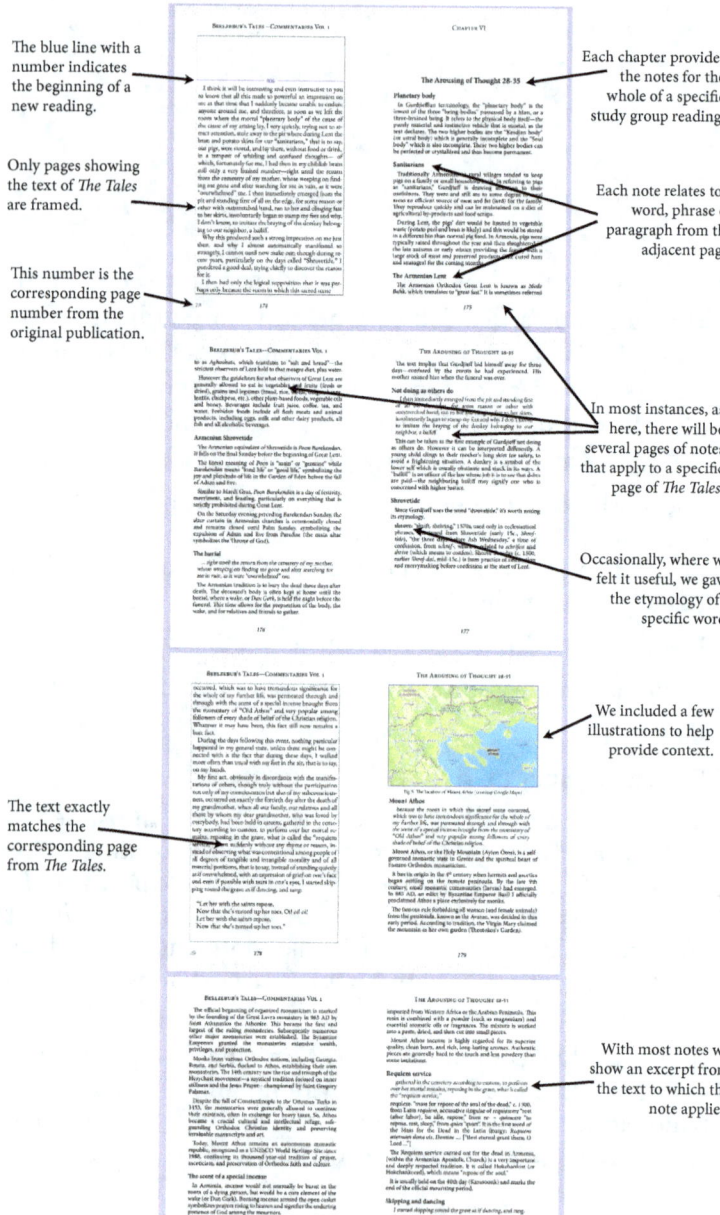

The blue line with a number indicates the beginning of a new reading.

Only pages showing the text of *The Tales* are framed.

This number is the corresponding page number from the original publication.

The text exactly matches the corresponding page from *The Tales*.

Each chapter provides the notes for the whole of a specific study group reading.

Each note relates to a word, phrase or paragraph from the adjacent page.

In most instances, as here, there will be several pages of notes that apply to a specific page of *The Tales*.

Occasionally, where we felt it useful, we gave the etymology of a specific word.

We included a few illustrations to help provide context.

With most notes we show an excerpt from the text to which the note applies.

On the left hand page we provide a visual picture of how the book is laid out in an effort to clarify its structure to the reader.

The important points to note are:

- The book is divided into chapters, each of which correspond to a reading that was studied and discussed by the most recent Tales Study Group.

- The readings are numbered, 001, 002, 003 and so on. This book covers six readings, up to page 50 of *The Tales*.

- The original page from *The Tales* to which the notes apply always appears on a left hand page.

- The notes which apply to that page then begin on the right hand page and may go on for several pages using both left and right side pages. We then proceed to the next page of *The Tales*.

- Each note applies to a specific word, phrase, sentence or paragraph. With each note, in most cases, we also provide an excerpt from the text which mentions the topic of the note.

It is likely that, with time, this book and other volumes in the series will need to be updated. The editor realizes this and has made provision for it.

To provide, thoughts, ideas or contributions use the contact form on ToFathomTheGist.Com.

I hope this volume proves useful to you.

001

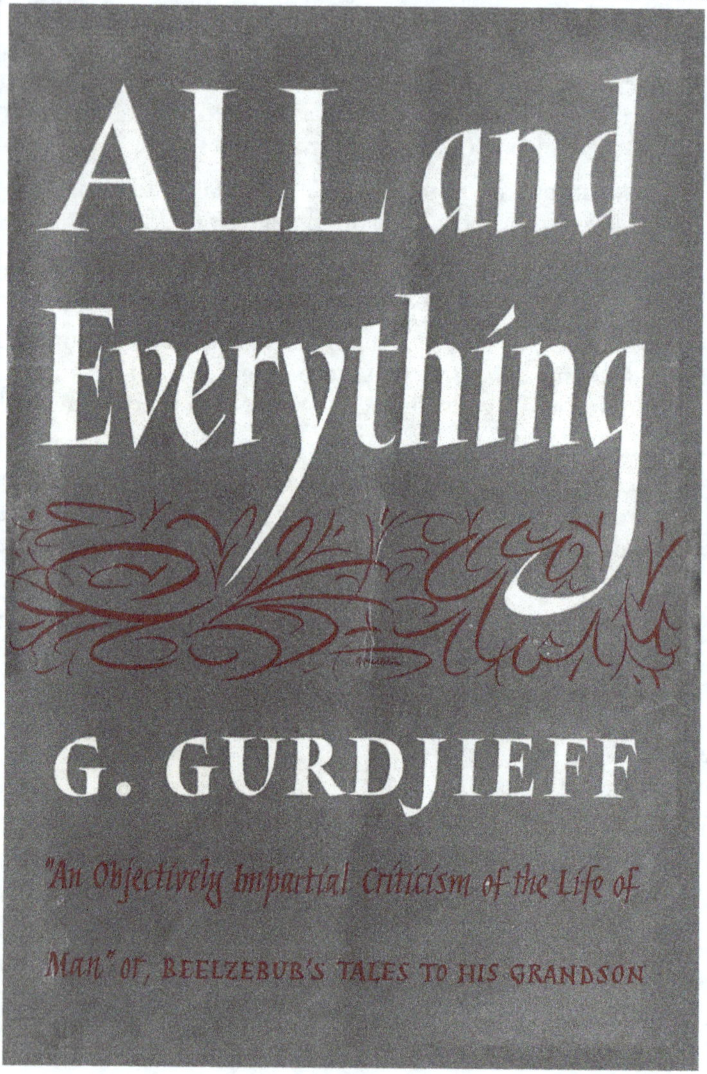

Fig 1. The original dust jacket cover of the first English edition of The Tales.

Chapter I

The Cover and Preface

The original cover

The opposite page shows a copy of the front face of the dust jacket of the first edition of The Tales.

It is possible, and in our view likely, that Gurdjieff himself determined to some degree the design of the dust jacket. One of us had a conversation about this with Paul Beekman Taylor, who was a child at the Prieuré. Taylor considered it possible that Gurdjieff designed that cover, noting that, at one time, Gurdjieff created a scrapbook for several of his children and illustrated the cover himself.

There are several anecdotal stories about Gurdjieff doing design work, including a reference in *Meetings with Remarkable Men* to drawing a monogram on a shield for a neighbor. So it is quite likely that Gurdjieff sketched out a design for the cover and gave it to someone to complete prior to publication.

The actual design was most likely done by Philip Grushkin, a relatively well known cover designer of that era. If you examine the cover on the page opposite closely, his signature can be found among the swirls below the book's title. For those who are interested, a Google search[1] will provide further information about him.

On the next page you will see an image of the front cover of the first German edition of the Tales. As you can see its form is very similar to the first English edition.

Let us consider this front page, line by line. The "main title" is:

ALL and Everything

---

[1] Search *"This Just In: Book Jackets by Philip Grushkin"* or *"Dust Jacket Designer Philip Grushkin From Comps To Final"*.

Fig 2. The original cover of the dust jacket of the first German edition of
The Tales.

Note the typography:

"ALL" is fully capitalized. We take capitalization to indicate something holy. It seems likely that it indicates OUR ENDLESSNESS as a unity. In contrast, only the first letter of "Everything" is capitalized. It seems likely that "Everything" represents the multiplicity of the Megalocosmos—the fractioning of the everything down to our level and beneath. We wrapped "main title" in quotes because ALL and Everything is not the title of the book, but the title of three series of books.

Gurdjieff's name

Gurdjieff's name is printed as G. GURDJIEFF, without the middle initial, and it is fully capitalized. This could be interpreted as normal typographic respect for the author. The font size is smaller than the title of the series, but, unusually, larger than the title(s) of the book itself.

We presume it to be an accidental error that subsequent editions of this book and all other books written by Gurdjieff list the author as G. I. Gurdjieff. This is the only edition of *The Tales* over which Gurdjieff had control of such details, and on the inside pages the name is also listed as G. GURDJIEFF. Gurdjieff had full control over the publication of *The Herald of Coming Good*, and everywhere his name is printed in that booklet it is G. GURDJIEFF.

The spine of the book just shows ALL and Everything and Gurdjieff's name, without mention of the series title.

The dual title

Next on the cover is the series title,

"An Objectively Impartial Criticism of the Life of Man" or, BEELZEBUB'S TALES TO HIS GRANDSON.

This is distinctly unusual, for three reasons. First, the font size is smaller than Gurdjieff's name. Second, it is not presented as a subtitle, since it does not follow the title ALL and Everything. And finally, there is not one title, but a dual title.

Dual titles for a book are rare. They were not so when Mary Shelley published *Frankenstein; or, The Modern Prometheus* in 1818. And they still occur occasionally as in: *Dr. Strangelove or: How I learned to stop worrying and love the bomb.* Or the play, *The Goat, or Who is Sylvia?* Literary convention designates the first of the two titles to be the real title and the second to be a subtitle. So, on occasion, publishers of Frankenstein have dropped the second part of the title. Nevertheless, the reality is that a dual title means whatever the author intended and thus should probably be left undisturbed.

Gurdjieff chose *"An Objectively Impartial Criticism of the Life of Man"* to be the primary title and BEELZEBUB'S TALES TO HIS GRANDSON to be the alternative. The only time he references the book without mentioning both titles is in the book itself, where he mentions just the primary title:

> "Or again, a being whose love resembled that of a contemporary terrestrial suitor for a rich widow—of course before he has received a single penny from her—would turn just as spiteful as one of those malicious persons who, foaming at the mouth, will hate that poor author who is now writing about you and me, in his work entitled An Objectively Impartial Criticism of the Life of Man.

The Tales p973

We note here that the primary title is wrapped in quotes and the alternative title is not. Since "An Objectively Impartial Criticism of the Life of Man" is not something some individual has said, these are shock quotes, indicating that Gurdjieff wishes us to ponder the meaning of these words.

"An Objectively Impartial Criticism of the Life of Man"

Objectively: The meaning of "objectively" is "in a way uninfluenced by personal feelings or opinions."

Impartial: The meaning of "impartial" is "fair and just."

Criticism: The meaning of "criticism," when it does not refer to a review of a literary or artistic work, is: "an expression of disapproval of someone or something based on perceived faults or mistakes." It has negative overtones. The etymology goes back to the Greek *kritikos* referring to someone who is able to make judgements.

Life of Man: In the juxtaposition of "Life" and "Man," the word "Man" clearly denotes human beings in general, and thus we can take "Life of Man" to denote not just the span of time between birth and death, but also how modern human beings in general live their lives.

So, taken together, we receive the impression that the book will discuss the faults and errors of modern man and will do so without being influenced by any of Gurdjieff's personal feelings or subjective opinions and it will do so in a just manner.

BEELZEBUB'S TALES TO HIS GRANDSON

Tale: A tale is a narrative or story that may be true or otherwise. It can be used in the sense of simply communicating (a statement), or entertaining the listeners (with a narrative), or teaching (as in recounting a fable).

Beelzebub: The choice of Beelzebub as the protagonist of the story is partly explained by Gurdjieff in the first chapter, so we will leave it until later in this book to discuss that.

Grandson: Some commentators have suggested that Beelzebub represents Gurdjieff and that his grandchildren are the modern people of the Work who were born too late to ever meet Gurdjieff and hence to whom he can only speak through his writings. This theory implies that Gurdjieff's immediate pupils were his children and their pupils and pupil's pupils are his grandchildren.

Because this title is capitalized, we are inclined to regard it as referring to a sacred collection of tales.

Or

One theory for the existence of two titles for the first series is that this series is, in reality, two books woven together.

The first book is, as the primary title suggests, a withering criticism of many aspects of the life of both historical and modern man. If you were so inclined, you could take note of every criticism that Beelzebub makes of priests, scientists, doctors, kings, emperors, politicians and so on, and you would have an inventory of human failings.

The second book is, as P. L. Travers called it in her memorable description of the book, published in *The Gurdjieff International Review*, a "great, lumbering flying cathedral." Its central arc is the flight of the *Karnak* and Beelzebub's recounting of his experiences with "the three-brained beings of planet Earth." It is an allegory, within which there are allegories, within which there are allegories. Included is a full creation myth and many obscurely described scientific ideas and information.

The first book is quite accessible to the reader who dares to persevere. The second book is where "the dog is buried."

In his book, *Gurdjieff: Making a New World*, J. G. Bennett writes:

> "If Gurdjieff had intended his meaning to be readily accessible to every reader, he would have written the book differently. He himself used to listen to chapters read aloud, and if he found that key passages were taken too easily—and therefore almost inevitably too superficially—he would rewrite them in order, as he put it, to "bury the dog deeper." When people corrected him and said that he surely meant "bury the bone deeper," he would turn on them and say it is not the 'bones' but the 'dog' that you have to find. The dog is Sirius, the dog star...

It's possible that Bennett is right that the dog is Sirius. However, there is another possibility. There is a German idiom "Da liegt der Hund begraben" (meaning "where the dog is buried") that would be obscure to most English readers, but might well have been familiar to Gurdjieff.

The Cover and Preface

G. GURDJIEFF

All and Everything

Ten Books in Three Series,
of which this is the First Series

The Cover and Preface

Original written in Russian and Armenian. Translations into other languages have been made under the personal direction of the author, by a group of translators chosen by him and specially trained according to their defined individualities, in conformity with the text to be translated and in relation to the philological particularities of each language.

The Philological Declaration

The copyright page

In the 1950 edition, the second page after the title page is the copyright page. It is on this page that we find what we have called "the philological declaration," hidden under the copyright notice:

We use the word "hidden" deliberately. This is important text, (Gurdjieff suggested it was important by also including it in *The Herald of Coming Good*), but Gurdjieff does not call attention to it at all—instead burying it on a left hand copyright page that few readers will even glance at—and it does not appear at all in the original German version.

It is one of Gurdjieff's "deceptions." Only the attentive reader will notice it and read it. And even the reader who does is unlikely to pay much attention to it, since on the surface all it seems to say is "I originally wrote it in Russian and Armenian, and I personally supervised the translation to ensure it was done well."

However, the reader needs to take note of the word "philology" and consider what Gurdjieff is saying.

Philology and meaning

Philology: The dictionary defines philology as "the branch of knowledge that deals with the structure, historical development, and relationships of a language or languages." This is a somewhat unsatisfactory definition in respect of "Gurdjieff's philology," since he had little respect for academic philologists. The etymology of "philology" is from the Greek *philologia* meaning "love of discussion, learning, and literature, or studiousness." This itself derives from *philo*, "loving" and logos, "word, speech."

Modern philology embraces linguistics (the scientific study of language and its structure). This is a 20th century addition to philology, of which Gurdjieff might disapprove. Philology can also be defined as "the study of literary texts, as well as oral and written records, the establishment of their authenticity and their original form, and the determination of their meaning."

Anecdotally Gurdjieff showed a strong interest in etymology, which is an indispensable part of philology in determining meaning. For example, if you know that a word only acquired a specific meaning in the 20th century and you encounter it in a 19th century text, you know to discard the 20th century meaning.

With *The Tales* we repeatedly encounter the need to explore the etymology of a word. In some contexts it is crucial. One example of this is: "The Law of Catching Up."

You will never determine its meaning if you do not examine its etymology. Its modern use is from sport and that meaning is now completely dominant, but it is not the meaning that Gurdjieff intends.

In summary

It appears that the philological declaration is simply a declaration that the book (which was originally written in Russian and Armenian) was translated with special attention to philology. Consequently, we need to pay special attention to philology when we read it.

The Cover and Preface

FIRST SERIES: Three books under the title of "An Objectively Impartial Criticism of the Life of Man," or, "Beelzebub's Tales to His Grandson."

SECOND SERIES: Three books under the common title of "Meetings with Remarkable Men."

THIRD SERIES: Four books under the common title of "Life is Real Only Then, When 'I Am.'"

All written according to entirely new principles of logical reasoning and strictly directed towards the solution of the following three cardinal problems:

FIRST SERIES: To destroy, mercilessly, without any compromises whatsoever, in the mentation and feelings of the reader, the beliefs and views, by centuries rooted in him, about everything existing in the world.

SECOND SERIES: To acquaint the reader with the material required for a new creation and to prove the soundness and good quality of it.

THIRD SERIES: To assist the arising, in the mentation and in the feelings of the reader, of a veritable, non-fantastic representation not of that illusory world which he now perceives, but of the world existing in reality.

The First Preface Page

Ten books in three series

The title page of *The Tales* states that *All and Everything* comprises ten books divided into three series. The first series consists of three books, the second of three books and the third of four books. This is a glaring inexactitude. Gurdjieff published *The First Series* at the end of his life and made arrangements for the later publishing of the first book of *The Second Series* and the first book of *The Third Series*.

So there are five official books, while Gurdjieff states unambiguously there will be ten, and does so on the first page of each book in the series, as shown opposite, with the exception of *Meetings With Remarkable Men*.

Gurdjieff was precise in his use of language and in his choice of words. This becomes very clear as you become more familiar with his writing. So we note that the second series, where we only know of one book, and the third series, where we only know of one book, are described as "under the common title," whereas the first series is described simply as "under the title."

So, what are the other books under these common titles? There is little evidence of them. The image on the next page is from the first page of a typewritten draft of chapter six of *Meetings With Remarkable Men*.

It suggests that the title of the book was not decided at the time, and that at least two books were intended. We can speculate that the three chapters beginning with *Ekim Bey* formed the second book, and perhaps that the final chapter, *The Material Question*, formed the third book. Unless some further evidence emerges, this is only speculation.

```
      E K K I M    B E Y

The first chapter of the second book of the second series--
MEN I HAVE KNOwN  BY  Georges Gurdjieff

For Mary Buckley
Copied by B.B.Rosett
February 1944.
```

The third series book *Life Is Real Only Then, When 'I Am'* has three clear sections: "The Prologue," a series of talks given by Gurdjieff to Orage's New York group and a final chapter entitled "The Inner and Outer Worlds of Man." There isn't any way to represent it as four books. And with this book, there is also the mystery of the missing chapters.

Missing chapters (or books)

At three different points in *Meetings with Remarkable Men*, Gurdjieff announces the titles of three chapters that he claims will be included in the third series. These chapters do not appear.

The chapter titles he promises are:

The physical body of man, its needs according to law, and possibilities of manifestation;

The astral body of man, its needs and possibilities of manifestation according to law; and

The divine body of man, and its needs and possible manifestations according to law.

The following entry appears in the book *Gurdjieff and The Women of the Rope.*

Thursday, June 18 1936

Lunch. We read the entire Skridloff chapter and all of us were deeply moved by the last part, especially the talk of Father Giovanni about understanding, faith, etc. Last night Gurdjieff told Alice that the last three portraits in his "gallery"- Karpenko, Dr. Ekim Bey, and Skridloff, from which three full books will flow, represent the astral body of man.

It seems that this is what Gurdjieff intended, but there is no evidence of such books.

An unwritten book

In *The Tales* on page 917 we read of another book which he suggests he might write, with a footnote that contains the following words:

Note: If anyone is very interested in the ideas presented in this chapter, I advise him to read, without fail, my proposed book entitled The Opiumists, if, of course, for the writing of this book there will be sufficient French armagnac and Khaizarian bastourma.

THE AUTHOR

As far as we are aware, there is no evidence that this book was ever completed, or even begun.

New principles of logical reasoning

Having described the three series, he declares these books to be:

All written according to entirely new principles of logical reasoning...

It could be argued that Gurdjieff is exposing the reader to unfamiliar forms of reasoning. To claim that he is employing entirely new principles of logical reasoning seems an excessive claim, but as he does not explain what he means by this, it could conceivably be true, given that this is a book like no other.

Cardinal problems

He directs this logical reasoning towards what he describes as three cardinal problems:

cardinal: This means "chief, principal or pivotal." Its etymology is curious. It comes from the Latin *cardo* meaning "hinge, pivot, key." The summer solstice was cardo anni, the turning point of the year. The pole star is the cardo of the sky. There are cardinal sins and cardinal virtues.

Gurdjieff does not specifically state what the problems are. Instead he includes their description in his proposed solution. We can state the problems as follows:

1st Problem: The beliefs and views, rooted in the reader over centuries, about everything existing in the world, hinder or prevent his evolution.

Solution: Destroy them.

Gurdjieff states unambiguously that people are awash with unhelpful beliefs and views and he intends, with this first series, to destroy such beliefs and views, freeing the reader from their influence.

2nd Problem: The reader requires appropriate material in order to create a new way of being.

Solution: Provide the material.

Gurdjieff sees the second series as constructive, and in it he intends to provide guidelines on how to live.

3rd Problem: The reader needs to perceive the world as it is.

Solution: Help him (in his mentation and his feelings).

The first and second series sets the reader on a particular course. However, Gurdjieff implies that these alone will not be enough to bring the reader into direct contact with reality as it is. The purpose of the third book is to make this possible.

THE COVER AND PREFACE

Friendly Advice

[Written impromptu by the author on delivering this book, already prepared for publication, to the printer.]

ACCORDING TO the numerous deductions and conclusions made by me during experimental elucidations concerning the productivity of the perception by contemporary people of new impressions from what is heard and read, and also according to the thought of one of the sayings of popular wisdom I have just remembered, handed down to our days from very ancient times, which declares:

"Any prayer may be heard by the Higher Powers and a corresponding answer obtained only if it is uttered thrice:

Firstly—for the welfare or the peace of the souls of one's parents.

Secondly—for the welfare of one's neighbor.

And only thirdly—for oneself personally."

I find it necessary on the first page of this book, quite ready for publication, to give the following advice:

"Read each of my written expositions thrice:

Firstly—at least as you have already become mechanized to read all your contemporary books and newspapers.

Secondly—as if you were reading aloud to another person.

And only thirdly—try and fathom the gist of my writings."

Only then will you be able to count upon forming your own impartial judgment, proper to yourself alone, on my writings. And only then can my hope be actualized that according to your understanding you will obtain the specific benefit for yourself which I anticipate, and which I wish for you with all my being.

AUTHOR

The Friendly Advice

Friendly

The page entitled "Friendly Advice" is placed immediately before the contents page in the 1950 edition. We presume the word "friendly" is to indicate that you will be grateful for the advice given, if you follow it. However, few people have the discipline to follow it.

An inexactitude

This page begins with:

> [Written impromptu by the author on delivering this book, already prepared for publication, to the printer.]

In reading the sentence we get the impression that Gurdjieff, delivering the final draft of the book for publication, suddenly thought: "Hmm, maybe I should add a little advice at the beginning on how to read the book." Deciding it was a good idea he immediately dashed off a few paragraphs and added them at the beginning of the manuscript. This could not have been the case.

Even if we imagined that there were a process by which an author could turn up to the printer and quickly add an extra page to the soon-to-be-printed manuscript (there isn't), we would know without doubt that the sentence was untrue. This is because Gurdjieff printed this page of Friendly Advice with these same words in square parentheses in *The Herald of Coming Good*, which was published in 1933, 16 years before the final manuscript of *The Tales* was delivered.

Usually, the use of square parentheses around text indicates that the text is added by someone other than the author. This is obviously not the case here. It suggests that the whole page was an afterthought.

Another possibility, however, is that the sentence is true. This possibility stems from the etymology of "impromptu."

impromptu: In normal usage the word "impromptu" means "without being planned" or "without being rehearsed." However, etymologically, it comes from the Latin *in promptu*, which means "in readiness," implying that the performer of the act was "ready," even if the act itself was not preconceived.

We can also consider the meaning of the word "on."

On: It will be a surprise to most readers that the preposition "on" has twelve possible meanings. They are as follows:

01. "in physical contact with"—as in "she was lying on the floor."

02. "forming a part of"—as in "she had a scratch on her arm."

03. "as a member of"—as in "she served on the board."

04. "having something as a target or focus"—as in "she kept her eyes on the prize."

05. "having something as a medium of storage or transmission"—as in "she stored his name on her computer."

06. "in the course of"—as in "she was on her way."

07. "indicating the day or part of a day when an event occurred"—as in "she did it on Thursday morning."

08. "engaged in"—as in "she was on an errand."

09. "regularly taking"—as in "she was on a course of antibiotics."

10. "will be paid for by"—as in "the drinks are on her."

11. "added to"—as in "the sales tax put a few cents on the price."

12. "having as a topic"—as in "the author wrote his advice on delivering the book to the printer."

Meaning 12 is the most likely meaning to apply if we want to take Gurdjieff's words literally. The intended meaning would then be that the friendly advice was written in readiness, on the topic of delivering the book to the printer.

What is heard and read

Next we encounter the words:

According to the numerous deductions and conclusions made by me during experimental elucidations concerning the productivity of the perception by contemporary people of new impressions from what is heard and read ...

Here Gurdjieff declares that he is very familiar with people's perceptions of new impressions in respect of listening and reading, and that he has conducted experiments to understand the process. We should have little doubt that this is the case, given the many reports of him having *The Tales* read out and observing the reaction of the audience.

We then read:

... and also according to the thought of one of the sayings of popular wisdom I have just remembered, handed down to our days from very ancient times, which declares:

"Any prayer may be heard by the Higher Powers and a corresponding answer obtained only if it is uttered thrice:

Firstly—for the welfare or the peace of the souls of one's parents.

Secondly—for the welfare of one's neighbor.

And only thirdly—for oneself personally."

Here Gurdjieff implies that there is a correspondence between the thought behind this ancient saying and the reading of *The Tales*, which relates specifically to prayer. He implies that there is a correspondence between the three objects of prayer: for the welfare or the peace of the souls of one's parents, for the welfare of one's neighbor and for oneself personally, and the three modes of reading the book, which he is about to describe.

How to read *The Tales*

In a few paragraphs Gurdjieff provides his advice on how to read *The Tales* and all his other books. The word "quite" as in "quite ready" can be taken to mean "thoroughly."

Firstly

> ... at least as you have already become mechanized to read all your contemporary books and newspapers.

Even diligent readers read mechanically. It is not done mindlessly—clearly information is absorbed—but it is done without a great deal of attention. It is perhaps worth noting here that *The Tales* defeats some people. They are not able to complete a first reading of the book.

Gurdjieff sees a parallel between reading mechanically and praying:

> ... for the welfare or the peace of the souls of one's parents.

It may be easier to understand this if we refer to one of Gurdjieff's comments about one's parents:

> All religions, all teachings come from God and speak in the name of God. This does not mean that God actually gave them, but they are connected with one whole and with what we call God.

> For example: God said, Love thy parents and thou wilt love me. And indeed, whoever does not love his parents cannot love God. Before we go any further, let us pause and ask ourselves. Did we love our parents, did we love them as they deserved, or was it simply a case of "it loves," and how should we have loved?

Gurdjieff's Early Talks p174

The advice is to read "at least as you have already become mechanized to read" in the same way that one might pray "at least mechanically." Many of our mechanisms are bequeathed to us by our parents. We owe them.

Secondly

> ... as if you were reading aloud to another person...

On the surface of it, this is "an exercise" and not an easy one to carry out. We can read the book aloud to another person, or read it aloud when we are alone, but it is, in our opinion, more difficult to read "as if out loud." And, incidentally, to do this we need to understand the typography and Gurdjieff's rhythm as a writer and how to pronounce the neologisms.

Those who are experienced in reading aloud to others will know that, when one does so, one splits one's attention between the act of reading and the act of listening to the words as you utter them. You attempt to consider the listener and you try to be eloquent. This is a distinctly different and, for some, unusual way of reading a book. It is a three-centered activity. The thinking center parses the words on the page, the voice (controlled by the moving center) is modulated by the emotional center and yet no sound is made. Control of one's breathing is also involved.

Gurdjieff sees a parallel between reading in this way and praying:

> ... for the welfare of one's neighbor ...

This may be easier to appreciate if we refer to the following words that appear in *The Tales*:

> ... the commandment inculcated in me in my childhood, enjoining that "the highest aim and sense of human life is the striving to attain the welfare of one's neighbor," and that this is possible exclusively only by the conscious renunciation of one's own.

> *The Tales* p1186

In order to read out loud effectively, one needs to be a willing and faithful servant to the listeners.

Thirdly

And only thirdly—try and fathom the gist of my writings.

First, we note that Gurdjieff writes: "And only thirdly," advising that there should be no attempt to "try and fathom the gist" in either of the other two modes of reading.

If the intended meaning of "try and fathom the gist" is "try to fathom the gist" it is bad English, which is not at all likely. Even if Gurdjieff were capable of making such an error, he had Alfred Orage as his editorial assistant, who would never have allowed such an elementary grammatical error to pass without comment.

try: Consider the etymology of "try." The original meaning of this word is from the Anglo-French *trier* which meant "to examine judiciously or sit in judgement of" and from which comes the English word "trial." It only later acquired the meaning of "to attempt to do."

fathom: The noun "fathom" is a measure of six feet, which approximates to the length of arms stretched out sideways from finger tip to finger tip. The verb "fathom," from Old English, means "to embrace, surround, envelop," giving the sense of "getting your arms around." It later came to mean "to get to the bottom of."

gist: This is of French origin. Gîte is French for a "domicile or habitation" and also has the meaning of something "covert." An associated verb from Old French, gésir gives gist en (third person present indicative), meaning "it consists in" or "lies in." The "gist" thus came to mean "the heart of" or "the essence of."

To "try and fathom the gist" speaks of two efforts, not one. To sit in judgement over and to get to the essence.

Gurdjieff sees a parallel between reading in this way and praying:

And only thirdly—for oneself personally.

One way of thinking about the parallel between this three-part prayer and the reading of *The Tales* is to think of it in terms of body, essence and reason. The second reading is for growth of essence. The third reading is for growth of Reason (i.e. not ordinary reason).

Only then

Gurdjieff concludes this page with:

Only then will you be able to count upon forming your own impartial judgment, proper to yourself alone, on my writings. And only then can my hope be actualized that according to your understanding you will obtain the specific benefit for yourself which I anticipate, and which I wish for you with all my being.

These words imply a promise. As far as the reader is concerned, if he reads it in the manner described, he will be able to form his own "impartial judgement"—a rare capacity the reader probably never possessed before reading the book——and Gurdjieff's hope for the reader, the nature of which he does not specifically state, will be actualized.

CONTENTS

Contents Pages

The themes of *The Tales*

The Tales embodies multiple interweaving themes and arcs. In non-fiction books there is usually a single linear theme. In fictional work there can be several interweaving themes with a sub-plot here and there, but it is rare to have more than three interweaving themes.

A good example of three interweaving fictional themes is provided by Shakespeare's play *A Midsummer Night's Dream*, where the action passes between the dispute among the fairies between Oberon and Titania, the encounters between the four "lovers" who enter the forest and the villagers (the mechanicals) who are rehearsing a play to perform at the court. These themes intersect and ultimately they all resolve happily.

The Tales can't be classified as a work of fact or fiction as it is a hybrid of both. And remarkably there are many more themes than you are likely to find in any other work. We believe it is worth enumerating and describing all these themes here, with reference to the list of contents.

Direct Teaching: The Preface pages, Chapters 1, "The Arousing of Thought," and "Chapter 48, From The Author" are direct teaching by Gurdjieff that partly prepare the reader for reading the book. This is supplemented at various points throughout.

Beelzebub's misbehavior, Exile and Redemption: This is one of the major themes of the first series, beginning in Chapter 2 and supplemented in many chapters that explain how Beelzebub redeemed himself until, in

Chapter 47, "The Inevitable Result of Impartial Mentation," is fully redeemed and perfected.

Mullah Nassr Eddin's Teaching. In many places throughout the first series, Mullah Nassr Eddin offers words of wisdom. These can be viewed as the observations of an impartial witness. This is similar if not identical to the role of the fool in some of Shakespeare's plays.

Beelzebub's Tales to Hassein. This theme is set up in Chapter 3, "The Cause of the Delay in the Falling of the Ship *Karnak*"—a justification is given for Beelzebub to begin his education of Hassein, and this continues in the many chapters that describe Beelzebub's visits to Earth, his interactions with Gornahoor Harharkh and with angels and archangels.

The Journey of the *Karnak*. The journey of the *Karnak* proceeds initially from Beelzebub's home planet, Karatas, for Beelzebub to attend a conference and then return. The action on the *Karnak* is referred to in various chapters. The final event is described in Chapter 47, "The Inevitable Result of Impartial Mentation."

The Heavenly Realm. Incidentally at various times, we encounter the appearances, actions and explanations of various high individuals; angels, archangels, cherubim and seraphim.

The History of Mankind. The history of mankind is told from Atlantis (Chapter 15, "The First Descent of Beelzebub upon the Planet Earth" up to the present day). There is much in this that is allegorical, to the point where it could also be viewed as depicting the life of a single man.

Messengers from Above. Ashiata Shiemash (Chapters 25, 26, and 27) occupies the central role among all the mentioned messengers sent from above, but others are also discussed. This theme complements the theme of the descent of mankind.

Kundabuffer and The Descent of Mankind: The primary difficulty for humanity is depicted as being a result of an error (the implanting of Kundabuffer) on the part of a

commission of archangels. Strongly associated with this are the behaviors of various Hasnamuss individuals, which could be the subject of a study in its own right.

Beelzebub's Sojourns. The sojourns tell stories of their own. We can examine what prompted each sojourn (Chapters 15, 19 - 24, 31) and how Beelzebub interfered in the affairs of men or simply observed them.

Gurdjieff's Travels: It will likely be noticed by the reader that Beelzebub's path on his sixth sojourn roughly follows Gurdjieff's path from central Asia through Russia, Germany and France, and finally to America.

Transspace Ships. This particular area of study involves considering the meaning of the various forms of transport which can be viewed allegorically as various changes of state, or means of self-observation. Connected with this are Beelzebub's various activities on Saturn and Mars.

HIS ENDLESSNESS and the Creation. Chapter 39, 'The Holy Planet "Purgatory,"' contains the primary description of the creation, depicting its origin as being a struggle between the Heropass and HIS ENDLESSNESS. This sets up a cosmology which can be taken as the foundation of Objective Science.

Objective Science. There are many references throughout *The Tales* to aspects of Objective Science. It starts in Chapters 4, 5 and 6, the last of which seems to be a description of the enneagram. At many places the laws of Heptaparaparshinokh and Triamazikamno are described, and the concept of the Trogoautoegocrat is introduced. Okidanokh is also described and discussed.

How Should Men Live? Beelzebub sees the prevalence of war (reciprocal destruction) and man's use of electricity as central problems for man that need to be resolved. Beelzebub's final words could be regarded as his suggested solution.

How to Work on Oneself. At various points important ideas about the physical and psychic life of man are elucidated and helpful advice is provided.

※

FIRST BOOK

※

The Cover and Preface

The Arousing of Thought

A MONG other convictions formed in my common presence during my responsible, peculiarly composed life, there is one such also—an indubitable conviction—that always and everywhere on the earth, among people of every degree of development of understanding and of every form of manifestation of the factors which engender in their individuality all kinds of ideals, there is acquired the tendency, when beginning anything new, unfailingly to pronounce aloud or, if not aloud, at least mentally, that definite utterance understandable to every even quite illiterate person, which in different epochs has been formulated variously and in our day is formulated in the following words: "In the name of the Father and of the Son and in the name of the Holy Ghost. Amen."

That is why I now, also, setting forth on this venture quite new for me, namely, authorship, begin by pronouncing this utterance and moreover pronounce it not only aloud, but even very distinctly and with a full, as the ancient Toulousites defined it, "wholly-manifested intonation"—of course with that fullness which can arise in my entirety only from data already formed and thoroughly rooted in me for such a manifestation; data which are in general formed in the nature of man, by the way, during his preparatory age, and later, during his responsible life engender in him the ability for the manifestation of the nature and vivifyingness of such an intonation.

Having thus begun, I can now be quite at ease, and should even, according to the notions of religious morality existing among contemporary people, be beyond all doubt assured that everything further in this new venture of mine will now proceed, as is said, "like a pianola."

Chapter II

The Arousing of Thought 3-9

Common presence

Among other convictions formed in my common presence...

Throughout *The Tales*, Gurdjieff uses such terms as "common presence." "common cosmic harmony," and so on as if they are terms which the reader is familiar with when they are not. The casual reader is likely to gloss over such terms without considering their meaning. In this example, "common presence" describes objectively the normal presence of man as being common between his three brains.

Indubitable conviction

an indubitable conviction...

The tendency to pronounce aloud "In the name of the Father and of the Son and in the name of the Holy Ghost. Amen" when commencing something new is not a common habit. Such a pronouncement is a Christian practice, generally known as the Trinitarian formula. Clearly, it invokes the Holy Trinity—one God existing as three distinct Persons: the Father, the Son (Jesus Christ), and the Holy Ghost (or Holy Spirit).

This behavior is performed in many different contexts, both formal and informal:

The Sign of the Cross: This is the most common use. Many Christians (especially Catholic, Orthodox, Anglican, and Lutheran) say these words while touching their forehead, chest, and shoulders, as a personal prayer, a blessing, or at the beginning and end of a prayer.

Baptism: It is the essential formula for a valid Christian Baptism. Jesus instructs his disciples in the Gospel of Matthew (28:19) to *"go and make disciples of all nations, baptizing them in the name of the Father and of the Son and of the Holy Spirit."* This is the origin of the Trinitarian formula.

Beginning and Ending Prayer: It is often used to open or close both personal prayers and formal liturgical services, such as the Catholic Mass.

Blessings: A priest or minister will often use this formula when giving a final blessing to the congregation.

Sacraments: It is used in other sacraments, such as during the absolution of sins during Confession.

The Trinitarian formula dedicates the action being started (whether it's a prayer, a baptism, or simply starting a task) to God. It sets the moment or act apart as something holy—done for God's glory.

Oddly, Gurdjieff writes the formula incorrectly:

> *"In the name of the Father and of the Son and in the name of the Holy Ghost. Amen."*

—adding an additional and unexpected *"in the name of."* He clearly did so deliberately, perhaps simply to startle the reader.

Ancient Toulousites

> as the ancient Toulousites defined it, *"wholly-manifested intonation"*...

There is little historical record of Toulouse prior to 118 BCE, when it became part of the Roman Empire. That status continued until 418 CE, when Visigoths took control of the area. They were succeeded by Merovingian Franks, then Carolinian Franks. All were Christian cultures in some form, as was the Cathar religion, which dominated Toulouse for a while in the 13th century.

Catharism was deemed heretical by the Catholic Church, and Pope Innocent III launched a crusade, known as the Albigensian Crusade, with the intention of wiping out

Catharism completely. This culminated with the surrender of Montségur, the last major Cathar stronghold, after a lengthy siege by French royal forces that had begun in May 1243. Subsequently, two hundred Cathars who refused to renounce their faith were burned to death. It is said that they threw themselves into the flames singing hymns. This could be what Gurdjieff is referring to as a "wholly manifested intonation."

This crusade also had a political dimension, as it offered a pretext for the French Crown and northern French barons to conquer the wealthy, culturally distinct, and politically independent lands of the Languedoc. The lords of the Languedoc, particularly the Counts of Toulouse, were accused of being too tolerant of (or even protecting) the Cathars.

The etymology of the word "define" is worth noting:

define: late 14c., *deffinen, diffinen,* "to specify; to fix or establish authoritatively." From Old French *defenir, definir* "to finish, conclude, come to an end; bring to an end; define, determine with precision," and directly from Medieval Latin *diffinire, definire,* from Latin *definire* "to limit, determine, explain."

Toulouse and Triamazikamno

In his book, *The Teachings of Gurdjieff, A Pupil's Journal* (p104-105) C.S. Nott describes a talk given by Gurdjieff with the following words:

He had been writing in the garden, and came to where some of us were sitting at the tables outside the dining room. He began to speak about Triamazikamno, the Law of Three, of the three forces, three principles. The only thing I remembered of this talk was his reference to the ancient Toulousites. Later, discussing this, one of the pupils drew a diagram of a symbol in the cathedral at Toulouse. It may be seen in some English churches.

As we studied it, we saw the connexion between the diagram and the Athanasian Creed. The Creed is a discourse on the Law of Three —at least the first part is; and the diagram is a symbol of that which is far older than Christianity. And now the Creed took on quite a different meaning from the literal one I had heard as a boy—that all those who did not believe in it, in the Church's sense, were actually condemned to suffer in hell.

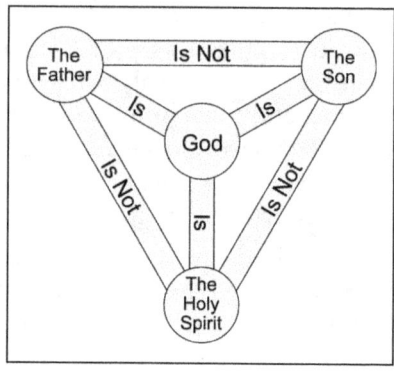

Notions of religious morality

according to the notions of religious morality existing among contemporary people...

The word "morality" refers to the principles concerning the distinction between right and wrong or good and bad behavior. Etymologically, it comes from the Late Latin word *morālitās*, which meant "manner, character, proper behavior." The contemporary religious morality Gurdjieff invokes here is the Christian view.

Like a pianola

everything further in this new venture of mine will now proceed, as is said, "like a pianola."

He implies that, according to the principles of religious morality, his writing of books will proceed "like a pianola,"— meaning "automatically without any effort on his part."

Pianola: A pianola, more commonly known as a player piano, is a self-playing piano. The original such automated musical instruments contained a pneumatic or electro-mechanical mechanism that read music from a perforated paper roll (often called a "piano roll"). As the roll unwound, the holes in the paper passed over a sensor bar, which triggered the mechanism to strike the corresponding keys on the piano.

This is clearly meant ironically since the writing of a book consciously could never be achieved in a mechanical fashion.

In any case I have begun just thus, and as to how the rest will go I can only say meanwhile, as the blind man once expressed it, "we shall see."

First and foremost, I shall place my own hand, moreover the right one, which—although at the moment it is slightly injured owing to the misfortune which recently befell me—is nevertheless really my own, and has never once failed me in all my life, on my heart, of course also my own—but on the inconstancy or constancy of this part of all my whole I do not find it necessary here to expatiate—and frankly confess that I myself have personally not the slightest wish to write, but attendant circumstances, quite independent of me, constrain me to do so—and whether these circumstances arose accidentally or were created intentionally by extraneous forces, I myself do not yet know. I know only that these circumstances bid me write not just anything "so-so," as, for instance, something of the kind for reading oneself to sleep, but weighty and bulky tomes.

However that may be, I begin ...

But begin with what?

Oh, the devil! Will there indeed be repeated that same exceedingly unpleasant and highly strange sensation which it befell me to experience when about three weeks ago I was composing in my thoughts the scheme and sequence of the ideas destined by me for publication and did not know then how to begin either?

This sensation then experienced I might now formulate in words only thus: "the-fear-of-drowning-in-the-overflow-of-my-own-thoughts."

To stop this undesirable sensation I might then still have had recourse to the aid of that maleficent property existing also in me, as in contemporary man, which has become inherent in all of us, and which enables us, with-

Gurdjieff's use of quotation marks

The Tales abides by English punctuation conventions to denote speech, alternating from double quotes to single quotes when there is speech within speech (i.e., when Beelzebub is speaking but relating what someone else said).

Quotes are also often used by Gurdjieff when giving names to things in a list, as in the following excerpt:

> ... *These new movements of painting are known there by the names of 'cubism,' 'futurism,' 'synthesism,' 'imagism,' 'impressionism,' 'colorism,' 'formalism,' 'surrealism,' and many other similar movements, whose names also end in 'ism.'*

We suspect that, in this instance, the quotes could have been left out from the sentence without damaging the meaning that Gurdjieff intended. However, in other situations, the quotes are there for a different purpose. It can be regarded as bad style to emphasize a word using quotes—boldface or underlining is more normal—but Gurdjieff, and/or his editors, chose to use quotes frequently for that purpose.

When he uses quotes in that manner, he is indicating that we should pay specific attention and not apply our mechanized associations in assigning meaning to them.

There is potential for confusion between these two uses of quotes. That may be intended, because it obliges the reader to pay attention all the time. In many situations it simply is not obvious why he uses quotes. For example, in Chapter 42, "Beelzebub in America," we read the following:

> "*In general he always drank more than enough of the 'alcoholic liquids' existing there;*

We are obliged to wonder what he means by applying quote-marks to "alcoholic liquids." The first time we encounter such quote-marks we might simply think of it as an aspect of Gurdjieff's quirky writing style, but if we are familiar with English punctuation we will realize that they are scare quotes.

Scare quotes: Scare quotes, which are also known as sneer quotes or shudder quotes, signal that the writer is distancing himself from the normal meaning of the word or phrase enclosed in the quotation marks. It's a way for the writer to show they are using a term with skepticism, irony, or to imply it's a term, the meaning of which the reader should ponder. For example, the writer may use quotes to show that this is what other people call something, not what the writer calls it.

Hand on heart

The gesture of placing one's right hand on one's heart generally implies honesty, sincerity, and truthfulness.

Gurdjieff's accident

In 1924, G.I. Gurdjieff was in a near-fatal car accident in France while driving from Paris to his institute at the Château du Prieuré in Fontainebleau. He was driving his Citroën, reportedly at high speed, when he lost control and crashed violently into a tree. He was found unconscious and suffered severe injuries, including a serious concussion, remaining unconscious for several days.

Two well-written books that offer perspectives and details about this event are: *Boyhood with Gurdjieff* by Fritz Peters, and *Our Life with Mr. Gurdjieff* by Thomas and Olga de Hartmann. Gurdjieff claims that because of this accident, he has been forced to write and confesses that he has no desire to do so. Although he doesn't directly state it, the implication is that events have forced him to pass on knowledge through writing rather than through other means that he had planned.

Bulky tomes

I know only that these circumstances bid me write not just anything "so-so," as, for instance, something of the kind for reading oneself to sleep, but weighty and bulky tomes.

The reader is clearly aware that *The Tales* is a long book split into three volumes. Whether Gurdjieff wrote this sentence before he knew how lengthy his book would be is impossible to know, as it is well recorded that he wrote and rewrote this first chapter many times.

Tome: The word tome has its roots in the act of "cutting." It traces back directly from the Middle French tome, which was taken from the Latin tomus. The Latin tomus was borrowed from the Ancient Greek word τόμος (tómos), which meant "a piece cut off," "a section," or "a part of a book."

The connection is that in the ancient world, large works were often written on long papyrus scrolls. A single, complete work might be too large for one scroll, so it was "cut" into several smaller, more manageable rolls. Each individual scroll or "section" of the larger work was called a *tómos*.

How to begin

This sensation then experienced I might now formulate in words only thus: "the-fear-of-drowning-in-the-overflow-of-my-own-thoughts."

Since Gurdjieff has taken *ALL and Everything* as the subject as his book, it seems likely that he could become overwhelmed with ideas of what to write and how to write it, to the point where deciding how to begin is a challenge.

out experiencing any remorse of conscience whatever, to put off anything we wish to do "till tomorrow."

I could then have done this very easily because before beginning the actual writing, it was assumed that there was still lots of time; but this can now no longer be done, and I must, without fail, as is said, "even though I burst," begin.

But with what indeed begin ... ?

Hurrah! ... Eureka!

Almost all the books I have happened to read in my life-have begun with a preface.

So in this case I also must begin with something of the kind.

I say "of the kind," because in general in the process of my life, from the moment I began to distinguish a boy from a girl, I have always done everything, absolutely everything, not as it is done by other, like myself, biped destroyers of Nature's good. Therefore, in writing now I ought, and perhaps am even on principle already obliged, to begin not as any other writer would.

In any case, instead of the conventional preface I shall begin quite simply with a Warning.

Beginning with a Warning will be very judicious of me, if only because it will not contradict any of my principles, either organic, psychic, or even "willful," and will at the same time be quite honest—of course, honest in the objective sense, because both I myself and all others who know me well, expect with indubitable certainty that owing to my writings there will entirely disappear in the majority of readers, immediately and not gradually, as must sooner or later, with time, occur to all people, all the "wealth" they have, which was either handed down to them by inheritance or obtained by their own labor, in the form of quieting notions evoking only naive dreams,

A preface

The word "preface" comes from the Old French *preface,* which in turn comes from the Late Latin *praefatia.* This Latin word is a compound of two parts: *prae*: meaning "before," and *fari* (or its noun form *fatia*): meaning "to speak."

So, the literal etymological meaning of "preface" is "something spoken before." It was originally used to describe the introductory part of a prayer or speech, and later came to mean the introduction to a book or other written work.

Gurdjieff's use of capitalization

With both the words Nature and Warning, Gurdjieff capitalizes the first letter. This is unusual and should be noticed by the reader.

Proper nouns, i.e., names for languages, nationalities, days, months, laws, planets, countries, towns, streets and people, should be capitalized in normal written English. Aside from these, and adjectives deriving from them, the only other grammatically sanctioned uses of capitalization are at the beginning of sentences and in the use of common nouns when they are used to denote an entire class of things as in: "What a piece of work is Man."

So Gurdjieff's use of capitalization violates the usual rules of grammar. In *The Tales* he capitalizes words to emphasize their meaning, seeming to imply that they relate to a spiritual level rather than a mundane level. In these two examples Nature could be thought of as Nature in its sacred role as part of the creation, and Warning could be construed as a warning to the higher part of your psyche. Later in *The Tales* we will note the capitalization of Being, and Reason, and note that these two words are not always capitalized.

It is also notable that Gurdjieff capitalizes all the neologisms (new words) he invents and uses throughout *The Tales,* and, of course, names for the Absolute, such as OUR ENDLESSNESS, are fully capitalized.

Not as it is done by...

> I have always done everything, absolutely everything, not as it is done by other, like myself, biped destroyers of Nature's good.

This is the first time that Gurdjieff points out his tendency to behave in creative and original ways. In making this claim, he also makes his first direct criticism of man, as a destroyer of Nature's good.

Triples

In the text, throughout *The Tales* Gurdjieff mentions three term groups (we refer to these as triples). He begins with Father, Son and Holy Ghost, and on this page he refers to:

> my principles, either organic, psychic, or even "willful,"

Meaning presumably, "of the body or the mind or the emotions." Note that willful is wrapped in quotes. Later (on page 8) he includes another triple:

> "psycho-physico-astrological" investigation

The warning

The Warning is clearly an outlandish exaggeration.

> ... both I myself and all others who know me well, expect with indubitable certainty that owing to my writings there will entirely disappear in the majority of readers, immediately and not gradually, as must sooner or later, with time, occur to all people, all the "wealth" they have, which was either handed down to them by inheritance or obtained by their own labor, in the form of quieting notions evoking only naive dreams, and also beautiful representations of their lives at present as well as of their prospects in the future.

While it is true that most if not all readers of *The Tales* encountering the book for the first time are imbued with quieting notions and unrealistic representations of both their current and future existence, no book is going to puncture that fantasy instantly or even quickly. Nevertheless, reading *The Tales* can and in some cases does have a devastating effect on one's worldview.

and also beautiful representations of their lives at present as well as of their prospects in the future.

Professional writers usually begin such introductions with an address to the reader, full of all kinds of bombastically magniloquent and so to say "honeyed" and "inflated" phrases.

Just in this alone I shall follow their example and also begin with such an address, but I shall try not to make it very "sugary" as they usually do, owing particularly to their evil wiseacring by which they titillate the sensibilities of the more or less normal reader.

Thus ...

My dear, highly honored, strong-willed and of course very patient Sirs, and my much-esteemed, charming, and impartial Ladies—forgive me, I have omitted the most important—and my in no wise hysterical Ladies!

I have the honor to inform you that although owing to circumstances that have arisen at one of the last stages of the process of my life, I am now about to write books, yet during the whole of my life I have never written not only not books or various what are called "instructive-articles," but also not even a letter in which it has been unfailingly necessary to observe what is called "grammaticality," and in consequence, although I am now about to become a professional writer, yet having had no practice at all either in respect of all the established professional rules and procedures or in respect of what is called the "bon ton literary language," I am constrained to write not at all as ordinary "patented-writers" do, to the form of whose writing you have in all probability become as much accustomed as to your own smell.

In my opinion the trouble with you, in the present instance, is perhaps chiefly due to the fact that while still in childhood, there was implanted in you and has now become ideally well harmonized with your general psyche, an excellently working automatism for perceiving all kinds

Wiseacre

Prior to Gurdjieff's writing, the word "wiseacre" was not frequently employed. It's an Old English word dating back to the late 1590s, and it has Dutch origins. It was borrowed from the Middle Dutch *wijssegger*, which meant "soothsayer" or "prophet" (literally, a "wise-sayer"). The Dutch word itself was likely a modification of the Old High German word *wizzago* (or *wissago*), which also meant "prophet" or "wise person." This root is related to the Old English *witan* ("to know"), which also gives us the word "wit."

However, English speakers, borrowing the unfamiliar Dutch *wijssegger*, corrupted the ending to -acre, and assigned it a different meaning. While the original Dutch and German words meant "wise person," the English word was always used contemptuously to mean "one who pretends to be wise," a "know-it-all," possibly a racial insult to the Dutch.

The not so "sugary" address

My dear, highly honored, strong-willed and of course very patient Sirs, and my much-esteemed, charming, and impartial Ladies—forgive me, I have omitted the most important—and my in no wise hysterical Ladies!

This is direct sarcasm. Most "Sirs" are neither strong-willed nor patient and the "Ladies" unlikely to be impartial and likely to be prone to hysteria at times. Readers who are unfamiliar with Gurdjieff may already be getting the impression that Gurdjieff is high-handed and arrogant. And it is likely that he wished to make such an impression, to alienate those who would anyway find *The Tales* too difficult to navigate. From the very beginning the book requires an unusual level of effort from the reader.

Grammar and grammaticality

While in ancient times grammars were created both for Sanskrit and Greek they mainly focused on simply defining parts of speech. Modern grammars have their origin in Latin grammar that was formulated in the Middle Ages in Europe.

Latin grammar came into existence in an effort to standardize the use of the language, which was no longer a spoken language anywhere. Nevertheless it was very much a written language and problems arose because it had become the written language of academia, and it was extensively used by the Catholic Church. There was a great deal of diversity in written Latin, to the extent it could easily be misinterpreted.

So, the adoption of a formal Latin grammar was intended to resolve that problem, and it did. Grammar-schools, first founded in the late 14th century, were originally schools for learning Latin.

Academically, the idea that all languages needed grammatical rules caught on and thus, by the late 16th century, academics began to formulate grammars for other languages, including English.We can note here what the elderly Persian says in *Meetings With Remarkable Men (p10)* which is as follows:

'Strange as it may seem to you, in my opinion a great deal of harm to contemporary literature has been brought about by grammars, namely, the grammars of the languages of all the peoples who take part in what I call the "common malphonic concert" of contemporary civilization.

'The grammars of their different languages are, in most cases, constructed artificially, and have been composed and continue to be altered chiefly by a category of people who, in respect of understanding real life and the language evolved from it for mutual relations, are quite "illiterate".

So academics started to apply grammar to German, French, English and other languages. The problem with applying rules to how a language is spoken or written is that such rules are unenforceable. People don't obey the rules and the language evolves under the force of its usage.

Gurdjieff advised: "Know and use not the language of grammar, but the language of psychic associations." It seems from the text of *The Tales* that this is the grammar that

Gurdjieff uses, in the sense that many of his long paragraphs introduce unexpected and yet meaningful associations.

The "bon ton literary language"

> ... in respect of what is called the "bon ton literary language,"

"Bon ton" is a French phrase that means "good tone" or "good style." It normally refers to the fashionable, sophisticated, and "well-bred" manners and tastes of high society. When applied to literature it generally refers to modes of writing that are elegant, polished, sophisticated, witty, and articulate. As with most other things writing styles are subject to fashion.

Patented writers

> ... I am constrained to write not at all as ordinary "patented-writers" do, ...

We can take "patented writers" as irony, to describe authors who establish a subjective style which appeals to the modern reader. If their books sell, they are likely to repeat and repeat, "exercising their patent."

An objective assertion

> In my opinion the trouble with you, in the present instance, is perhaps chiefly due to the fact that while still in childhood, there was implanted in you and has now become ideally well harmonized with your general psyche, an excellently working automatism for perceiving all kinds of new impressions, thanks to which "blessing" you have now, during your responsible life, no need of making any individual effort whatsoever.

The assertion that Gurdjieff makes here is likely to be correct in respect of every reader. And he is warning the reader that effort is going to be required to read his book.

of new impressions, thanks to which "blessing" you have now, during your responsible life, no need of making any individual effort whatsoever.

Speaking frankly, I inwardly personally discern the center of my confession not in my lack of knowledge of all the rules and procedures of writers, but in my nonpossession of what I have called the "bon ton literary language," infallibly required in contemporary life not only from writers but also from every ordinary mortal.

As regards the former, that is to say, my lack of knowledge of the different rules and procedures of writers, I am not greatly disturbed.

And I am not greatly disturbed on this account, because such "ignorance" has already now become in the life of people also in the order of things. Such a blessing arose and now flourishes everywhere on Earth thanks to that extraordinary new disease of which for the last twenty to thirty years, for some reason or other, especially the majority of those persons from among all the three sexes fall ill, who sleep with half-open eyes and whose faces are in every respect fertile soil for the growth of every kind of pimple.

This strange disease is manifested by this, that if the invalid is somewhat literate and his rent is paid for three months in advance, he (she or it) unfailingly begins to write either some "instructive article" or a whole book.

Well knowing about this new human disease and its epidemical spread on Earth, I, as you should understand, have the right to assume that you have acquired, as the learned "medicos" would say, "immunity" to it, and that you will therefore not be palpably indignant at my ignorance of the rules and procedures of writers.

This understanding of mine bids me inwardly to make the center of gravity of my warning my ignorance of the literary language.

In self-justification, and also perhaps to diminish the

The three sexes

The insistence that there are three sexes continues throughout the book. (Male, female, and those who are neither one nor the other sex.)

Sleep with half-open eyes

... especially the majority of those persons from among all the three sexes fall ill, who sleep with half-open eyes and whose faces are in every respect fertile soil for the growth of every kind of pimple.

What Gurdjieff means by "sleeping with eyes half-open" is not clear. A more common expression is "sleeping with one eye open" implying that the person is never fully relaxed and feels the need to be vigilant. Sleeping with eyes half open might also refer to the waking sleep in which man spends most of his life.

The words "whose faces are in every respect fertile soil for the growth of every kind of pimple" imply masturbation.

Some "instructive article"

The urge to write novels (or instructive articles) in 1930s America was more common than in preceding decades. It was fueled by a unique combination of mass literacy, a deep national crisis that demanded explanation, a captive audience with time to read, and, for the first time, a government program that financially supported writing as a job.

It is reasonable to characterize such activity as a disease, since the vast majority of such books are never published or are self-published out of vanity and rarely read.

Disease

Currently, the medical world does not believe that pimples are a consequence of masturbation. The hormones, testosterone and progesterone can increase oil production which can clog pores, but there is no proven link between testosterone or progesterone levels and masturbation.

In any event, Gurdjieff's assertion makes metaphorical sense in this context, as aspiring authors who have little to offer in their writings are most likely devoted to self-aggrandizement ...

This strange disease is manifested by this, that if the invalid is somewhat literate and his rent is paid for three months in advance, he (she or it) unfailingly begins to write either some "instructive article" or a whole book.

invalid: "infirm or sickly person," 1709, originally of disabled military men. As an adjective, "not strong, infirm from sickness, disease, or injury", 1640s, from Latin *invalidus* "not strong, infirm, impotent, feeble, inadequate," from *in* "not" + *validus* "strong."

The manifestation of the disease is that someone becomes an aspiring author if they have some literary skill—skill in the use of the "bon ton literary language"—and have no immediate need to earn money. The quotes around "instructive article" are clearly ironic.

Well knowing about this new human disease and its epidemical spread on Earth, I, as you should understand, have the right to assume that you have acquired, as the learned "medicos" would say, "immunity" to it,

"medico": "medical practitioner," 1680s, from Spanish *médico* or Italian *medico*, from Latin *medicus* "physician; healing."

"immunity": late 14c., "exemption from service or obligation," from Old French *immunité* "privilege; immunity from attack, inviolability" (14c.) and directly from Latin *immunitatem* "exemption from performing public service or charge, privilege," from *immunis* "exempt, free, not paying a share." Medical sense of "protection from disease" is from 1879, from French or German.

Gurdjieff's preference for the quoted "medico" rather than physician is interesting. The quoting of "medico" and "immunity" probably indicates a metaphorical use of the words, as what he is describing is not a disease in the normal sense of the word.

... and that you will therefore not be palpably indignant at my ignorance of the rules and procedures of writers.

This understanding of mine bids me inwardly to make the center of gravity of my warning my ignorance of the literary language.

palpable: late 14c., "that can be touched," from Latin *palpabilis* "that may be touched or felt," from Latin *palpare* "touch gently, stroke." Figurative sense of "easily perceived, evident" also is from late 14c.

indignant: 1580s, from Latin *indignantem* "impatient, reluctant, indignant," present participle of *indignari* "to be displeased at, be offended, resent, deem unworthy," from *indignus* "unworthy."

Gurdjieff employs many words to warn the reader that the book they are about to read is going to have an unfamiliar style and will not be like anything they would normally encounter. On the first reading of *The Tales* in these early pages, this warning is likely to be skipped over and not taken in. However, it deserves the reader's attention.

In self-justification, and also perhaps to diminish the degree of the censure in your waking consciousness of my ignorance of this language indispensable for contemporary life, I consider it necessary to say,

censure: late 14c., "judicial sentence," originally ecclesiastical, from Latin *censura* "judgment, opinion," also "office of a censor," from *census*, past participle of *censere* "appraise, estimate, assess." General sense of "a finding of fault and an expression of condemnation" is from c. 1600.

This is curious. Gurdjieff rarely if ever cared what others thought of him, and thus these words have the character of intentional inexactitude, which should make us pay greater attention. From the context, "waking consciousness" seems to refer to our normal mechanical consciousness.

with a humble heart and cheeks flushed with shame, that although I too was taught this language in my childhood, and even though certain of my elders who prepared me for responsible life, constantly forced me "without sparing or economizing" any intimidatory means to "learn by rote" the host of various "nuances" which in their totality compose this contemporary "delight," yet, unfortunately of course for you, of all that I then learned by rote, nothing stuck and nothing whatsoever has survived for my present activities as a writer.

rote: c. 1300, "custom, habit," in phrase "by rote," "by heart," of uncertain origin. Possibly Middle English, from Anglo-French, of Germanic origin; akin to Old High German *hruozza* "crowd." Alternatively, sometimes said to be connected with Old French *rote* "route" or from Latin *rota* "wheel."

nuance: 1781, from French *nuance* "slight difference, shade of color" (17c.), from *nuer* "to shade," from *nue* "cloud," from Latin *nubes* "a cloud, mist, vapor" (source also of Latin *obnubere* "to veil," Welsh *nudd* "fog," Greek *nython*, in Hesychius "dark, dusky"). Possibly a reference to "the different colors of the clouds." that occurs particularly at dawn and dusk.

delight: c. 1200, *delit*, "high degree of pleasure or satisfaction," also "that which gives great pleasure," from Old French *delit* "pleasure, delight, sexual desire," from *delitier* "please greatly, charm," from Latin *delectare* "to allure, delight, charm, please," frequentative of *delicere* "entice." Spelled *delite* until 16c.; the modern unetymological form is by influence of light, flight, etc.

The words "taught this language in my childhood" now betrays something unexpected to the reader, as the reader will surely know (and if he doesn't he will soon discover it in the coming pages) that Gurdjieff did not learn English in his childhood, only Armenian and Greek. So the "bon ton literary language" he is referring to is not specific to any particular language; it refers to a way of using words internally and applying that to whatever language one speaks.

The phrase: "constantly forced me 'without sparing or economizing' any intimidatory means to 'learn by rote' the host of various 'nuances' which in their totality compose this contemporary 'delight'" may well have applied to Gurdjieff's upbringing, but probably also applied to our own.

Almost all of us came to use our language in a similar way, being "corrected" by parents and teachers, expecting discourse to observe particular forms, expecting written works to follow particular patterns. We became habitual in this. Gurdjieff claims he did not.

degree of the censure in your waking consciousness of my ignorance of this language indispensable for contemporary life, I consider it necessary to say, with a humble heart and cheeks flushed with shame, that although I too was taught this language in my childhood, and even though certain of my elders who prepared me for responsible life, constantly forced me "without sparing or economizing" any intimidatory means to "learn by rote" the host of various "nuances" which in their totality compose this contemporary "delight," yet, unfortunately of course for you, of all that I then learned by rote, nothing stuck and nothing whatsoever has survived for my present activities as a writer.

And nothing stuck, as it was quite recently made clear to me, not through any fault of mine, nor through the fault of my former respected and non-respected teachers, but this human labor was spent in vain owing to one unexpected and quite exceptional event which occurred at the moment of my appearance on God's Earth, and which was—as a certain occultist well known in Europe explained to me after a very minute what is called "psycho-physico-astrological" investigation—that at that moment, through the hole made in the windowpane by our crazy lame goat, there poured the vibrations of sound which arose in the neighbor's house from an Edison phonograph, and the midwife had in her mouth a lozenge saturated with cocaine of German make, and moreover not "Ersatz," and was sucking this lozenge to these sounds without the proper enjoyment.

Besides from this event, rare in the everyday life of people, my present position also arose because later on in my preparatory and adult life—as, I must confess, I myself guessed after long reflections according to the method of the German professor, Herr Stumpsinschmausen—I always avoided instinctively as well as automatically

The crazy lame goat

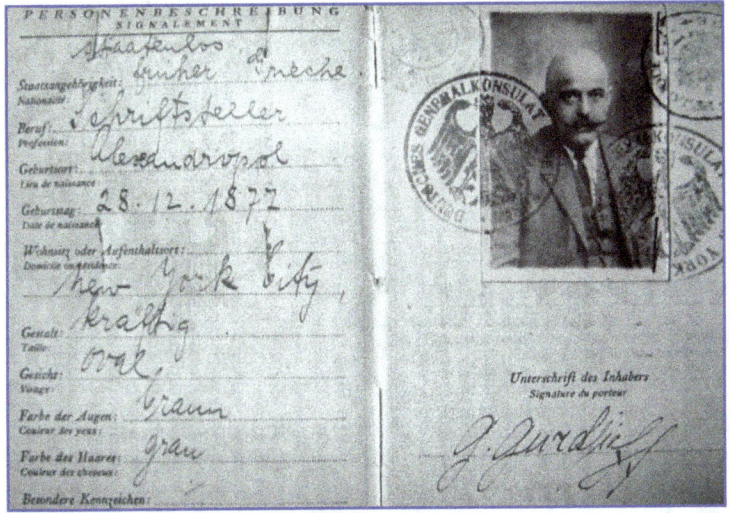

Fig 3. Gurdjieff's Passport

The passport shown above gives Gurdjieff's birth date as the 28th December 1877. The year 1877 is one of the three hypothesized birth years about which Gurdjieff's biographers debate. The two alternatives are 1866 and 1872 with the month and day usually given as January 13th. Some complexity is created by the fact that Gurdjieff reckoned dates by the Orthodox calendar rather than the European calendar.

January 13th is the date that most Gurdjieff groups choose to celebrate his birthday, for the simple reason that it is the date that Gurdjieff himself chose to celebrate his birthday. In *Meetings With Remarkable Men* on page 302 we read:

> Today is the tenth of January. Three days from now, by the old style calendar, the New Year will be welcomed in at midnight, an hour which is memorable for me as the time of my coming into the world.

The text is ambiguous as it could mean that the hour of midnight is memorable or that midnight on January 13th is memorable. January 10th corresponds to 28th December of the Orthodox calendar.

On this page (8) we encounter the words:

"... at that moment, through the hole made in the windowpane by our crazy lame goat, there poured the vibrations of sound which arose in the neighbor's house from an Edison phonograph, and the midwife had in her mouth a lozenge saturated with cocaine of German make, and moreover not "Ersatz," and was sucking this lozenge to these sounds without the proper enjoyment.

The crazy lame goat is a reference to Capricorn, Gurdjieff's star sign, whose symbol is the Sea Goat, a crazy lame goat of a kind. The hole made in the windowpane, in context, appears to mean the new year, which Capricorn (December 21st to January 20th) "kicks through," or ushers in every year.

The text, *there poured the vibrations of sound which arose in the neighbor's house from an Edison phonograph,* cannot have been factual. It can be taken as a reference to the fact that Gurdjieff was born in the same year that Edison invented the phonograph: 1877. In reality, the phonograph was not actively marketed until 1887.

The text, *and the midwife had in her mouth a lozenge saturated with cocaine of German make, and moreover not "Ersatz," and was sucking this lozenge to these sounds without the proper enjoyment,* is possibly a reference to the Russo-Turkish War of 1877-78 between the Ottoman Empire and the Eastern Orthodox coalition, led by Russia but including Bulgaria, Romania, Serbia and Montenegro.

That war which pervaded the area where Gurdjieff was born is thus designated as Gurdjieff's midwife. Russia declared war on 24 April 1877. The Russian army outnumbered the Turkish army, 300,000 to 200,000, but its weaponry was inferior. The Turkish army was armed with British and American-made rifles, which were superior in range to Russian rifles and it also possessed German-made (Krupps) artillery (the cocaine lozenge not properly enjoyed).

Despite their disadvantage, the Russians prevailed.

midwife: c. 1300, "woman assisting," literally "woman who is 'with'" (the mother at birth), from Middle English *mid* "with" + *wif* "woman."

ersatz: "inferior substitute," 1875, from German *Ersatz* "units of the army reserve," literally "compensation, replacement, substitute," from *ersetzen* "to replace," from Old High German *irsezzen*.

cocaine: alkaloid obtained from the leaves of the coca plant, 1874, from Modern Latin *cocaine* (1856), coined by Albert Niemann of Gottingen University from *coca* (from Quechua *cuca*) + chemical suffix *-ine*. A medical coinage, the drug was first used in the 1870s as a local anaesthetic for eye surgery, etc.

Herr Stumpsinschmausen

> as, I must confess, I myself guessed after long reflections according to the method of the German professor, Herr Stumpsinschmausen

The German word "schmausen" means feast. The meaning of "stumpsin" is less certain. It is close to, but is not, "stumpfsinn," which means dullness or apathy.

and at times even consciously, that is, on principle, employing this language for intercourse with others. And from such a trifle, and perhaps not a trifle, I manifested thus again thanks to three data which were formed in my entirety during my preparatory age, about which data I intend to inform you a little later in this same first chapter of my writings.

However that may have been, yet the real fact, illuminated from every side like an American advertisement, and which fact cannot now be changed by any forces even with the knowledge of the experts in "monkey business," is that although I, who have lately been considered by very many people as a rather good teacher of temple dances, have now become today a professional writer and will of course write a great deal—as it has been proper to me since childhood whenever "I do anything to do a great deal of it"—nevertheless, not having, as you see, the automatically acquired and automatically manifested practice necessary for this, I shall be constrained to write all I have thought out in ordinary simple everyday language established by life, without any literary manipulations and without any "grammarian wiseacrings."

An American advertisement

The modern era of illuminated advertising began in 1892 with the incandescent light bulb. The first illuminated billboard appeared in New York City, at the intersection of Broadway and 23rd Street, on the wall of the Cumberland Hotel near Madison Square. It was a real estate advert and used approximately 1,457 incandescent bulbs. It caused a sensation at the time, and was visible from far down Broadway.

Gurdjieff is not referring to neon signage which lights itself up. Neon signage was invented in France by Georges Claude in 1910 and didn't reach the U.S. until 1923.

Monkey business

The Oxford English Dictionary, suggests the term is a "calque" (a direct loan translation) of the Bengali word *bādrāmi*, which literally translates to "monkey-behavior" or "mischief."

The phrase first appeared in British print around 1835-1837. An 1837 letter by British Parliamentarian Thomas Perronet Thompson explicitly used the phrase in a colonial context, referring to actions that government officials wouldn't commit to, saying "no such 'monkey business' as the Indians call it."

It may be the case that Gurdjieff is designating Darwinian evolutionists as "experts in monkey business."

Simple everyday language

I shall be constrained to write all I have thought out in ordinary simple everyday language established by life ...

While it may not be very grammatical, the text of *The Tales* does not correspond to ordinary everyday language.

003

But the pot is not yet full! ... For I have not yet decided the most important question of all—in which language to write.

Although I have begun to write in Russian, nevertheless, as the wisest of the wise, Mullah Nassr Eddin, would say, in that language you cannot go far.

(Mullah Nassr Eddin, or as he is also called, Hodja Nassr Eddin, is, it seems, little known in Europe and America, but he is very well known in all countries of the continent of Asia; this legendary personage corresponds to the American Uncle Sam or the German Till Eulenspiegel. Numerous tales popular in the East, akin to the wise sayings, some of long standing and others newly

Chapter III

The Arousing of Thought 9-15

Mullah Nassr Eddin

Since Gurdjieff wrote the parenthesized words, Mullah Nassr Eddin has become far better known. There are now a number of websites devoted to collections of the Mullah's sayings, and also several books devoted to him by Idries Shah.

Mullah Nassr Eddin (also spelled Nasreddin, Nasrudin, and many other variants) is primarily considered a legendary or folkloric figure, though there is a strong tradition—particularly in Turkey—that claims he was a real historical person.

The most widely accepted version for his historical existence places him in 13th-century Anatolia (modern-day Turkey). It suggests he was born in the village of Hortu in 1208 and died in Akşehir in 1284. He is said to have been an educated Imam, and a qadi (judge). There is even a tomb in Akşehir that is attributed to him. It has a locked gate but no surrounding walls, a visual joke that fits the legend.

Irrespective of the truth of the legend, scholars have no doubt that the vast majority of the thousands of stories attributed to him are folklore that has accumulated over centuries.

Mullah Nassr Eddin represents the "wise fool," an archetype found in many cultures and also, a notable character in some of Shakespeare's plays.

Hodja

"Hodja" is an honorific title, that means "master" or "teacher," similar to "professor" or "reverend" in the West. It comes from the Farsi word *khwāja*, which means "lord" or "master." It is and was used widely through the Ottoman Empire and Persianate societies, and can be encountered across the Middle East, in the Balkans, and in Central Asia, and South Asia.

It should not be confused with the word "Hadji" (also Haji or Hajji) which is also an honorific title—an Islamic one—which comes from Arabic, and is a title of respect given to a Muslim who has successfully completed the Hajj, the obligatory pilgrimage to Mecca, which is one of the five pillars of Islam.

The title for a woman who has completed the Hajj is Hajjah.

Uncle Sam

"Uncle Sam" was originally the nickname of a real-life meatpacker, Samuel Wilson. During the War of 1812, Wilson secured a contract to supply barrels of beef to the U.S. Army. The barrels were required to be stamped with "U.S." to identify them as "United States" property. Some soldiers who knew Samuel Wilson referred to him as"Uncle Sam," and joked that the "U.S." stamp on the barrels actually stood for "Uncle Sam" Wilson. This caught on and the legend of Uncle Sam was born.

Uncle Sam is not generally regarded as a wise and humorous commentator like Mullah Nassr Eddin, but rather a personification of the U.S. government. He is generally thought of as an older man with white hair due to the image depicting him on the famous First World War recruitment poster.

Till Eulenspiegel

The character of the German Till Eulenspiegel is closer to that of Mullah Nassr Eddin, although he has no religious significance at all. Instead, he is generally thought of as a wandering peasant, a trickster and a jester, who spends his time exposing the foolishness and hypocrisy of everyone from craftsmen and innkeepers to priests, nobles, and even the Pope.

The name "Eulenspiegel," literally translates to "owl-mirror." He is an owl, holding up a mirror to society to expose its follies. The forename "Till" is a diminutive of the old Germanic Theodoric which means "ruler of the people."

Like Uncle Sam, Till Eulenspiegel was quite likely a real person, who became legendary. It is said that he was born in Kneitlingen near Brunswick around 1300 and is believed to have died of the Black Death in Mölln, Schleswig-Holstein, in 1350.

The first known collection of his adventures was published in a German book in 1515. Since then he has been the subject of many books, plays and musical works, most famously the 1895 tone poem "Till Eulenspiegel's Merry Pranks" by Richard Strauss.

In which language to write

Although I have begun to write in Russian, nevertheless, as the wisest of the wise, Mullah Nassr Eddin, would say, in that language you cannot go far.

The question: "In which language to write?" is likely to surprise the reader. Which author, other than Gurdjieff, would even ask such a question? Only a handful of authors would be capable of writing in more than one language, and any that were would most likely choose the one in which they had most practice.

Those who are monolingual, might even wonder whether it could make any difference. Only a multilingual person would know that some ideas that can be easily expressed in one language can sometimes not be expressed well in another that lacks the appropriate vocabulary. Gurdjieff provides his considered thoughts on the matter and clearly expects the reader to consider this question as well.

arisen, were ascribed and are still ascribed to this Nassr Eddin.)

The Russian language, it cannot be denied, is very good. I even like it, but ... only for swapping anecdotes and for use in referring to someone's parentage.

The Russian language is like the English, which language is also very good, but only for discussing in "smoking rooms," while sitting on an easy chair with legs outstretched on another, the topic of Australian frozen meat or, sometimes, the Indian question.

Both these languages are like the dish which is called in Moscow "Solianka," and into which everything goes except you and me, in fact everything you wish, and even the "after-dinner Cheshma"[1] of Scheherazade.

It must also be said that owing to all kinds of accidentally and perhaps not accidentally formed conditions of my youth, I have had to learn, and moreover very seriously and of course always with self-compulsion, to speak, read, and write a great many languages, and to such a degree of fluency, that if, in following this profession unexpectedly forced on me by Fate, I decided not to take advantage of the "automatism" which is acquired by practice, then I could perhaps write in any one of them.

But if I set out to use judiciously this automatically acquired automatism which has become easy from long practice, then I should have to write either in Russian or in Armenian, because the circumstances of my life during the last two or three decades have been such that I have had for intercourse with others to use, and consequently to have more practice in, just these two languages and to acquire an automatism in respect to them.

O the dickens! ... Even in such a case, one of the aspects of my peculiar psyche, unusual for the normal man,

---

[1] *Cheshma means veil*

Russian and English

The Russian language, it cannot be denied, is very good. I even like it, but ... only for swapping anecdotes and for use in referring to someone's parentage.

The Russian language is like the English, which language is also very good, but only for discussing in "smoking rooms," while sitting on an easy chair with legs outstretched on another, the topic of Australian frozen meat or, sometimes, the Indian question.

Gurdjieff compares Russian and English. Russian is the dominant Slavic language, and English is the dominant Germanic language. They employ some different sounds, they have quite different alphabets. They exhibit very different grammars and sentence structure and they have very few common words. Nevertheless, from Gurdjieff's perspective they are alike in their limitations as suitable languages in which to write *The Tales*.

The reference to parentage is, perhaps, "tongue in cheek." All Russian names consist of three distinct parts, used in the following specific order:

1. The Given Name. The "Christian name" given at childbirth: Ivan, Vanya, etc.

2. The Patronymic. This indicates the father's first name: The ending of the patronymic is gender-specific: For example, Ivanovich means son of Ivan, whereas Ivanovna means daughter of Ivan.

3. The Surname (family name). Most Russian surnames have gender-specific endings. So Mr. Dostoevsky for the male becomes Ms. Dostoevskaya for the female.

The standard formal and polite way to address colleagues, elders, or anyone you don't know well is to use both the Given Name and the Patronymic (e.g., "Ivan Ivanovich" or "Vanya Ivanovna").

Anecdote: This comes from the Greek word ἀνέκδοτα (*anekdota*), which literally means "things unpublished": *an-* ("not") *ekdotos* ("published" or "given out"). In general, anecdotes are simple but interesting stories.

So, an anecdote was originally something "not given out."

English smoking rooms were a feature of the Victorian and Edwardian eras, which persisted in the pre-war era in upper-class houses. They were specially designed rooms for smoking pipes and cigars. After dinner, gentlemen would congregate away from the ladies to have intellectual conversations. In general, these rooms were furnished with velvet curtains and decorated in a masculine way. Gentlemen would even change into a velvet smoking jackets and caps (velvet absorbs smoke).

Gurdjieff describes the posture (sitting on an easy chair with legs outstretched on another) of casual conversation and pontification, rather than any meaningful exchange. Wrapping "smoking rooms" in quotes suggests that any venue where casual intellectual conversation takes place applies. The "Indian question" and "Australian frozen meat" were issues of the day that English intellectuals chatted about in the 1930s.

The Indian question: Having conquered India, the British had the problem of administering it. It was the "jewel in the crown" of the British Empire. As well as spices, jewels and textiles, India had a huge population that could and did provide manpower for many things, including soldiering. The Indian question was whether Britain had a right to rule India and whether it could continue to maintain the ability to exploit and administer such a large population (hundreds of millions). It was even argued that Britain was "civilizing" India and had a duty to do so "for the Indians' sake." Such an idea is now laughable.

Australian frozen meat: From the late 1870s onwards, Britain shipped refrigerated meat from Australia and New Zealand. Both countries had small populations and could produce far more meat than was needed locally, while Britain's population was expanding and required a good deal of imported food. Shipping frozen meat halfway round the world seemed like an odd and imperfect solution, but it worked for many years.

Solianka,

Both these languages are like the dish which is called in Moscow "Solianka," and into which everything goes except you and me, in fact everything you wish, ...

Solianka is a thick spicy and sour Russian soup. It is the kind of dish to which leftovers are added. So, aside from the main ingredients,[1] anything unused in the kitchen is added to the pot.

Gurdjieff uses the metaphor of Solianka to make the point that the English and Russian languages notably exclude words and concepts that are required for discussing "you and me."

Cheshma

... and even the "after-dinner Cheshma"* of Scheherazade.

[* Cheshma means veil.]

Cheshma does not mean veil, as Gurdjieff suggests in his footnote.

Cheshma: The word "cheshma" (also spelled chashma or cheshmeh) originates from the Classical Persian language. Its etymology links directly to (čašm), the Persian word for "eye." The derived word, *cheshma,* acquired the primary meaning of a "spring" or "fountain"—conceptually, a place where water flows from the "eye" of the earth.

Scheherazade

Scheherazade is referred to several times in *The Tales.* Aside from page 10, her name is found on pages 251, 273, 351, and 617. Her name (from middle Persian) means "noble lineage" and she is the central character in *The 1001 Nights.*

In brief, the story is as follows:

---

[1] *Pickled cucumbers, pickle brine from the jar, olives, capers, tomatoes, onions, ham, sausage and other meats. It is served with sour cream. Can also be fish based.*

King Shahryar discovers one day that his wife has been unfaithful to him. He has her executed and, having lost faith in the fidelity of all women, he decides to marry a new virgin each day and then behead her the following day, so that no wife will ever be unfaithful to him again.

After he has killed an untold number of his one-day brides, Scheherazade, the vizier's daughter, volunteers to become his next wife. When she enters the king's chambers that night, she asks if she might bid one last farewell to her beloved sister, Dunyazade. The name Dunyazade means "child of the world." At Scheherazade's instruction, Dunyazade comes to the royal bedchamber each night and requests that her sister tell "one last story."

The king is spellbound by Scheherazade's first story, but the night is over before she completes it. He asks her to finish, but Scheherazade says there is no time because dawn is breaking and the king spares her life so that she might finish the story. The next night Scheherazade finishes the story and then, at her sister's insistence begins another exciting tale, which she again fails to finish. In this way the king keeps Scheherazade alive until 1000 stories have been told over 1001 nights. At that point Scheherazade tells the king that she has no tales left to tell him, but by then the king has fallen in love with her. He spares her life and makes her his queen.

The story of Scheherazade itself can be viewed as an allegory of the intellect's relationship to the higher emotional side.

The meaning of "after-dinner Cheshma"—the tears of Scheherazade perhaps—is not clear. The implication may be that these languages are good for formulating imaginary ideas about the inner world of man.

Whether that is the case or not, the text of *The Tales* was eventually rendered in English. However, Gurdjieff invented many new words (neologisms) to express concepts for which, we presume, there were no English words, or even appropriate phrases.

Fate

> *... if, in following this profession unexpectedly forced on me by Fate, I decided not to take advantage of the "automatism" which is acquired by practice, then I could perhaps write in any one of them.*

Fate: late 14c., "one's lot or destiny; predetermined course of life;" also "one's guiding spirit," from Old French *fate* and directly from Latin *fata*, neuter plural of *fatum* "prophetic declaration of what must be, oracle, prediction," thus the Latin word's usual sense, "that which is ordained, destiny, fate," literally means "thing spoken (by the gods)."

Gurdjieff states that the profession of author was forced on him by "Fate." (Note that "Fate" is capitalized for emphasis.) If we accept this declaration, then it seems to follow that his car accident was also fated.

Dickens

> *O the dickens! ...*

dickens: The word "dickens," used by Shakespeare in *The Merry Wives of Windsor* ("I cannot tell what the dickens his name is"), is most probably a shortened form of "devilkins," meaning "little devils."

has now already begun to torment the whole of me.

And the chief reason for this unhappiness of mine in my almost already mellow age, results from the fact that since childhood there was implanted in my peculiar psyche, together with numerous other rubbish also unnecessary for contemporary life, such an inherency as always and in everything automatically enjoins the whole of me to act only according to popular wisdom.

In the present case, as always in similar as yet indefinite life cases, there immediately comes to my brain—which is for me, constructed unsuccessfully to the point of mockery—and is now as is said, "running through" it that saying of popular wisdom which existed in the life of people of very ancient times, and which has been handed down to our day formulated in the following words: "every stick always has two ends."

In trying first to understand the basic thought and real significance hidden in this strange verbal formulation, there must, in my opinion, first of all arise in the consciousness of every more or less sane-thinking man the supposition that, in the totality of ideas on which is based and from which must flow a sensible notion of this saying, lies the truth, cognized by people for centuries, which affirms that every cause occurring in the life of man, from whatever phenomenon it arises, as one of two opposite effects of other causes, is in its turn obligatorily molded also into two quite opposite effects, as for instance: if "something" obtained from two different causes engenders light, then it must inevitably engender a phenomenon opposite to it, that is to say, darkness; or a factor engendering in the organism of a living creature an impulse of palpable satisfaction also engenders without fail non-satisfaction, of course also palpable, and so on and so forth, always and in everything.

Adopting in the same given instance this popular wisdom

Popular wisdom

Sayings of popular wisdom persist in cultures by virtue of an oral tradition—one that is self-preserving. Because such sayings are short they are easily memorized and often repeated. Many use rhythm, rhyme ("Haste makes waste"), alliteration ("Live and learn"), or vivid metaphors ("Don't count your chickens before they hatch"). These literary qualities increase their stickiness.

They exist in all languages and cultural traditions, and are the primary vehicle for passing down a culture's core beliefs, ethics, and practical wisdom. They teach children about virtues such as patience ("A watched pot never boils"), hard work ("No pain, no gain"), or caution ("Look before you leap").

When a person uses a proverb, they are not just stating their own opinion. They are summoning the collective, anonymous wisdom of their ancestors. This gives weight and authority to their argument, advice, or criticism.

A stick with two ends

... that saying of popular wisdom which existed in the life of people of very ancient times, and which has been handed down to our day formulated in the following words: "every stick always has two ends."

The origin of the saying "every stick always has two ends" is as stated part of the Russian oral tradition. Gurdjieff was not the first to commit it to writing. It can also be found in Dostoyevsky's novel *The Brothers Karamazov* and was even used by Lenin once, in one of his political essays.

Gurdjieff then writes:

In trying first to understand the basic thought and real significance hidden in this strange verbal formulation, there must, in my opinion, first of all arise in the consciousness of every more or less sane-thinking man the supposition that, in the totality of ideas on which is based and from which must flow a sensible notion of this saying, lies the truth, cognized by people for centuries, which affirms that every cause occurring in the life of man, from whatever phenomenon it arises, as one of two opposite effects of other causes, is in its turn obligatorily molded also into two quite opposite effects, as for instance: if "something" obtained from two different causes engenders light, then it must inevitably engender a phenomenon opposite to it, that is to say, darkness;

This is a complicated set of words that is likely to cause the reader to puzzle over their meaning. In essence it states that in general events can have two outcomes, one positive and the other negative. This might also be viewed as a rough formulation of the Law of Three.[1]

---

[1] The Tales p751

formed by centuries and expressed by a stick, which, as was said, indeed has two ends, one end of which is considered good and the other bad, then if I use the aforesaid automatism which was acquired in me thanks only to long practice, it will be for me personally of course very good, but according to this saying, there must result for the reader just the opposite; and what the opposite of good is, even every non-possessor of hemorrhoids must very easily understand.

Briefly, if I exercise my privilege and take the good end of the stick, then the bad end must inevitably fall "on the reader's head."

This may indeed happen, because in Russian the so to say "niceties" of philosophical questions cannot be expressed, which questions I intend to touch upon in my writings also rather fully, whereas in Armenian, although this is possible, yet to the misfortune of all contemporary Armenians, the employment of this language for contemporary notions has now already become quite impracticable.

In order to alleviate the bitterness of my inner hurt owing to this, I must say that in my early youth, when I became interested in and was greatly taken up with philological questions, I preferred the Armenian language to all others I then spoke, even to my native language.

This language was then my favorite chiefly because it was original and had nothing in common with the neighboring or kindred languages.

As the learned "philologists" say, all of its tonalities were peculiar to it alone, and according to my understanding even then, it corresponded perfectly to the psyche of the people composing that nation.

But the change I have witnessed in that language during the last thirty or forty years has been such, that instead of an original independent language coming to us from the remote past, there has resulted and now exists one,

Consequences for the reader

... if I use the aforesaid automatism which was acquired in me thanks only to long practice, it will be for me personally of course very good, but according to this saying, there must result for the reader just the opposite; and what the opposite of good is, even every non-possessor of hemorrhoids must very easily understand.

Briefly, if I exercise my privilege and take the good end of the stick, then the bad end must inevitably fall "on the reader's head."

Gurdjieff concludes that he cannot write this book using his established habitual ability with languages, because it will not benefit the reader.

Gurdjieff refers to hemorrhoids three other times in *The Tales*, first describing them as a characteristic trait of contemporary actors, secondly as a consequence of using contemporary toilets and finally as a characteristic of humans who belong to the middle-sex.

The deterioration of Armenian

Gurdjieff criticizes the Russian language as unsuitable for discussing philosophical questions. He rejects Armenian as impractical for contemporary notions, lamenting that the language has deteriorated.

Philologically, the Armenian language is considered highly unusual by linguists for several key reasons. While it is classified as being part of the large Indo-European family (which includes English, Spanish, Russian, and Hindi), it is unique within that family, forming its own independent branch, with no close "sister" languages.

It has a unique alphabet, and includes unique sounds, particularly in its use of ejective consonants. These are sharp, voiceless consonants formed by pushing air out using the vocal cords rather than the lungs.

which though also original and independent, yet represents, as might be said, a "kind of clownish potpourri of languages," the totality of the consonances of which, falling on the ear of a more or less conscious and understanding listener, sounds just like the "tones" of Turkish, Persian, French, Kurd, and Russian words and still other "indigestible" and inarticulate noises.

Almost the same might be said about my native language, Greek, which I spoke in childhood and, as might be said, the "taste of the automatic associative power of which" I still retain. I could now, I dare say, express anything I wish in it, but to employ it for writing is for me impossible, for the simple and rather comical reason that someone must transcribe my writings and translate them into the other languages. And who can do this?

It could assuredly be said that even the best expert of modern Greek would understand simply nothing of what I should write in the native language I assimilated in childhood, because, my dear "compatriots," as they might be called, being also inflamed with the wish at all costs to be like the representatives of contemporary civilization also in their conversation, have during these thirty or forty years treated my dear native language just as the Armenians, anxious to become Russian intelligentsia, have treated theirs.

That Greek language, the spirit and essence of which were transmitted to me by heredity, and the language now spoken by contemporary Greeks, are as much alike as, according to the expression of Mullah Nassr Eddin, "a nail is like a requiem."

What is now to be done?

Ah … me! Never mind, esteemed buyer of my wiseacrings. If only there be plenty of French armagnac and "Khaizarian bastourma," I shall find a way out of even this difficult situation.

Clownish potpourri

Pot-pourri: This word comes directly from the French *pot-pourri,* which literally translates to "rotten pot." This was a direct translation of the Spanish *olla podrida,* which also means "rotten pot." It was the name of a popular Spanish stew made from a wide variety of different meats and vegetables all cooked together for a long time. The "rotten" part likely referred to the slow-simmering process that broke down the ingredients. The idea that carried over into English was the idea of a mixture. Thus it came to mean a heterogeneous mixture of many different things in one pot. By the mid-18th century, this concept of a "mixture" was applied to the aromatic concoction we know today.

While most languages include loan words from other usually neighboring languages, the past 150 years introduced social and technological shifts that have had a profound and general impact on virtually all spoken languages.

While mass literacy and the printing press had the effect of standardizing languages, later technologies changed the speed and style of communication and lent new words to all languages to describe these new phenomena. For the first time, a single language—English—became the global lingua franca for business, science, and culture. This, combined with unprecedented levels of global migration, has led to two major outcomes:

- Nearly every language in the world has adopted a large number of English words.
- Human migration caused words from other languages to be added to the mix. English is particularly prone to adopting loan words.

Nail and requiem

are as much alike as, according to the expression of Mullah Nassr Eddin, "a nail is like a requiem."

requiem: "mass for repose of the soul of the dead," c. 1300, from Latin *requiem,* accusative singular of *requies* "rest

87

(after labor), repose," from *re*, intensive prefix + *quies* "quiet." It is the first word of the Mass for the Dead in the Latin liturgy: *Requiem æternam dona eis, Domine...* ["Grant them eternal rest, O Lord ..."]

While, on the surface, this comparison is amusing, it may also have a deeper meaning. You can take requiem to mean "a prayer for soul of the dead." "Nail" could imply "a coffin nail," linking directly to the destiny of the physical body as opposed to higher bodies. You might also associate "nail" to the Holy Nails used to crucify Christ. Nevertheless, the two things are not alike.

French armagnac

Gurdjieff writes:

> ... *If only there be plenty of French armagnac.*

Armagnac was Gurdjieff's chosen drink for toasting after meals and is strongly associated with his ritual "Toasting of the Idiots." It is the oldest and one of the most revered brandies in France, with its roots in the Gascony region of southwestern France.

It is first mentioned by Maître Vital Dufour, a cardinal and prior in Gascony who wrote a book, *To Keep Your Health and Stay in Good Form,* in 1310. It was thus initially extolled as a medicine, a health drink. It became a popular spirit much later.

Khaizarian bastourma

Gurdjieff continues:

> ... *and "Khaizarian bastourma,"*

Bastourma is salted and dried meat. Folklore suggests that it originated with nomadic horsemen from the Central Asian steppes. These horsemen preserved meat for their later consumption by placing slabs of it in their saddlebags. The constant pressure from their legs while riding would press out the moisture from the meat, and the horse's sweat would salt it.

The word "bastourma" is the Armenian name for the dish. This comes from the Turkish verb bastırmak, which means "to press" or "to squeeze."

To make bastourma, the pressed and salted meat is covered with a paste made from fenugreek, paprika, garlic, and other spices. It is associated with Armenian cuisine and the city of Kayseri (formerly Caesarea) in modern-day Turkey (hence the name Khaizerian). It is popular throughout the Middle East.

I am an old hand at this.

In life, I have so often got into difficult situations and out of them, that this has become almost a matter of habit for me.

Meanwhile in the present case, I shall write partly in Russian and partly in Armenian, the more readily because among those people always "hanging around" me there are several who "cerebrate" more or less easily in both these languages, and I meanwhile entertain the hope that they will be able to transcribe and translate from these languages fairly well for me.

In any case I again repeat—in order that you should well remember it, but not as you are in the habit of remembering other things and on the basis of which are accustomed to keeping your word of honor to others or to yourself— that no matter what language I shall use, always and in everything, I shall avoid what I have called the "bon ton literary language."

In this respect, the extraordinarily curious fact and one even in the highest degree worthy of your love of knowledge, perhaps even higher than your usual conception, is that from my earliest childhood, that is to say, since the birth in me of the need to destroy birds' nests, and to tease my friends' sisters, there arose in my, as the ancient theosophists called it, "planetary body," and moreover, why I don't know, chiefly in the "right half," an instinctively involuntary sensation, which right up to that period of my life when I became a teacher of dancing, was gradually formed into a definite feeling, and then, when thanks to this profession of mine I came in contact with many people of different "types," there began to arise in me also the conviction with what is called my "mind," that these languages are compiled by people, or rather "grammarians," who are in respect of knowledge of the given language exactly similar to those biped animals whom

Russian and Armenian

... I shall write partly in Russian and partly in Armenian, the more readily because among those people always "hanging around" me there are several who "cerebrate" more or less easily in both these languages, and I meanwhile entertain the hope that they will be able to transcribe and translate from these languages fairly well for me.

The quotes surrounding "hanging around" suggest that he is referring to several of his pupils. His quoted use of "cerebrate" is surprising, as he never uses this word again throughout *The Tales*. He frequently uses the words "mentate" and "mentation," which have the meaning "mental function" to indicate "cerebration" which means "brain function."

The writing of *The Tales*

Meanwhile in the present case, I shall write partly in Russian and partly in Armenian,

The detail of the way that *The Tales* was written, as far as we can tell from the literature of the Work[1] is as follows:

Gurdjieff would write while sitting in cafés and observing the behavior of others. He made notes in notebooks, none of which have come to light. He would then dictate from his notes, sometimes in Russian to Madame de Hartmann, who would type in Russian, and sometimes to Lily Galumnian, (aka Lily Chaverdian), who would type in Armenian. These were the primary two of his pupils who were "hanging around."

Subsequently, the text that was typed in Armenian (the language he preferred for discussing psychological and philosophical ideas) was then translated into Russian. All of the Russian text was translated on a word-by-word basis by Bernard Metz, who was fluent in both Russian and English. He had been told by Gurdjieff to provide a direct word-for-word translation—to not add or subtract anything. He was nevertheless obliged to understand and convey meaning by his word choices.

[1] *From records of Orage's New York Meetings and from The Gurdjieff Years 1929-1949, by Louise March, and from other sources.*

This literal translation was sent to Orage, whose role was to edit this into an acceptable style for reading. He shared this work with Jean Toomer. Both Orage and Toomer would go to the Prieuré with their drafts and spend time going through them with Gurdjieff to finalize the text.

Orage used the largest Oxford English Dictionary as his reference for meaning and etymology. We know this because that copy of the Oxford English Dictionary is now owned by Paul Beekman Taylor. It is clear from this book (Orage made pencil notes on the pages) that Gurdjieff checked the etymology of many of the words that were used in *The Tales*.

After the text was edited and a draft completed to Gurdjieff's satisfaction, Gurdjieff had chapters read out to audiences of English speakers and observed their reactions. He subsequently made edits in accordance with what he had observed.

A universal language?

Given the meticulous approach that Gurdjieff took in writing *The Tales*, it is worth discussing what language the final version of *The Tales* is written in. On the surface, the English version is in English give or take hundreds of neologisms, and the same goes for the German version.

It is worth pondering the following extracts from *In Search of the Miraculous* by P. D. Ouspensky.

"*People do not clearly realize to what a degree their language is subjective, that is, what different things each of them says while using the same words. They are not aware that each one of them speaks in a language of his own, understanding other people's language either vaguely or not at all, and having no idea that each one of them speaks in a language unknown to him.*

People have a very firm conviction, or belief, that they speak the same language, that they understand one another. Actually this conviction has no foundation whatever. The language in which they speak is adapted to practical life only.

People can communicate to one another information of a practical character, but as soon as they pass to a slightly more complex sphere they are immediately lost, and they cease to understand one another ..."[1]

Clearly if *The Tales* had been written in ordinary subjective language, the reader would have no possibility of receiving much of the knowledge Gurdjieff wished to convey.

Now consider the following words:

Someone asked him about the possibility of a universal language—in what connection I do not remember.

"A universal language is possible," said G., "only people will never invent it."

"Why not?" asked one of us.

"First because it was invented a long time ago," answered G., "and second because to understand this language and to express ideas in it depends not only upon the knowledge of this language, but also on being. I will say even more. There exists not one, but three universal languages.

The first of them can be spoken and written while remaining within the limits of one's own language. The only difference is that when people speak in their ordinary language they do not understand one another, but in this other language they do understand.

In the second language, written language is the same for all peoples, like, say, figures or mathematical formulae; but people still speak their own language, yet each of them understands the other even though the other speaks in an unknown language.

The third language is the same for all, both the written and the spoken. The difference of language disappears altogether on this level."[2]

In the opinion of Orage, *The Tales* is an objective work of art. In *The Teachings of Gurdjieff*, C. S. Nott quotes one of Orage's comments on *The Tales*, as follows:

[1] *In Search of the Miraculous by P D Ouspensky, p68*
[2] *In Search of the Miraculous by P D Ouspensky. p95-96*

'I don't propose to rewrite it,' he said. 'In fact, apart from general editing, I shall leave it as it is until, probably the final revision, whenever that may be. The book will take shape. It is full of ideas. As I see it, it is really an objective work of art, of literature of the highest kind; it is in the category of scripture. It seems that Gurdjieff planned it while he was lying in bed after the accident. It is consciously designed to have a definite effect on everyone who feels drawn to reading it. Anyone who tried to rewrite it would distort it.

In *In Search of the Miraculous* Ouspensky recalls Gurdjieff saying:

"In real art there is nothing accidental. It is mathematics. Everything in it can be calculated, everything can be known beforehand. The artist knows and understands what he wants to convey and his work cannot produce one impression on one man and another impression on another, presuming, of course, people on one level. It will always, and with mathematical certainty, produce one and the same impression.

"At the same time the same work of art will produce different impressions on people of different levels. And people of lower levels will never receive from it what people of higher levels receive. This is real, objective art. Imagine some scientific work—a book on astronomy or chemistry. It is impossible that one person should understand it in one way and another in another way. Everyone who is sufficiently prepared and who is able to read this book will understand what the author means, and precisely as the author means it. An objective work of art is just such a book, except that it affects the emotional and not only the intellectual side of man."

It seems likely then that Gurdjieff's approach to creating *The Tales* was not only to produce a book that was objective (as he titled it, *An Objectively Impartial Criticism of the Life of Man*) but one that was written in the first universal language. As he personally oversaw the production of the English and the

German versions, we may assume that these two versions at least are texts written in the first universal language.

To destroy birds' nests

In this respect, the extraordinarily curious fact and one even in the highest degree worthy of your love of knowledge, perhaps even higher than your usual conception, is that from my earliest childhood, that is to say, since the birth in me of the need to destroy birds' nests, and to tease my friends' sisters, ...

The "high-sounding" start to this sentence is probably best taken literally. He states that what he is about to write is not just extraordinary and curious, but important knowledge. And then he notes that he had a "need" (rather than simply an inclination) to "destroy birds' nests" and "tease his friends' sisters," which was born in him in "earliest childhood."

The attention to his "friends' sisters" implies sexual interest. But what does destroying birds' nests imply? While some adolescent boys become rebellious and exhibit antisocial and even criminal behavior, not all do. It is hard to imagine such behavior as a need, and destroying birds' nests seems like an unlikely way of characterizing it. So it may have a metaphorical meaning.

In *The Tales*, birds (the raven inhabitants of Saturn, including Gornahoor Harhark and Gornahoor Rakhoorkh) signify the intellect. So perhaps destroying birds' nests signifies the common adolescent behavior of challenging intellectual authority in science and religion.

Ancient Theosophists

... there arose in my, as the ancient theosophists called it, "planetary body," ...

There are occasional mentions of the "planetary body" in modern theosophical writings, although the term is most often used to apply to the body of a planet rather than of a human being.

The modern theosophical movement is not at all ancient. It was established with the founding of the Theosophical Society on November 17, 1875, in New York City. Founding members included: Helena Petrovna Blavatsky, Colonel Henry Steel Olcott and William Quan Judge.

The word "theosophia," meaning "divine wisdom," was coined by Ammonius Saccas of Alexandria in the third century A.D. However, we can find no evidence of the mention of "planetary body" in the writings of the Neo-Platonists (ancient Theosophists), whom Ammonius Saccas inspired.

The right half

... chiefly in the "right half," an instinctively involuntary sensation, which right up to that period of my life when I became a teacher of dancing, was gradually formed into a definite feeling, and then, when thanks to this profession of mine I came in contact with many people of different "types," there began to arise in me also the conviction with what is called my "mind," ...

The right half of the body is under control of the left half of the brain, which is generally classified as the "intellectual" side. In the Gospel, the right side signifies the side of personality as in Matthew 5:29- 5:30:

And if thy right eye offend thee, pluck it out, and cast it from thee: for it is profitable for thee that one of thy members should perish, and not that thy whole body should be cast into hell.

And if thy right hand offend thee, cut it off, and cast it from thee: for it is profitable for thee that one of thy members should perish, and not that thy whole body should be cast into hell.

Sensation, feeling, conviction

Gurdjieff describes an involuntary sensation from child-hood which evolved into a feeling which ultimately became a conviction. He is, incidentally, describing a psychological process of development: sensations can invoke feelings which eventually form convictions in the mind.

Types

What Gurdjieff means precisely by types is unclear, even though he mentions it many times. As far as we are aware he never taught about "personality types," as described in the many popular books on this. Nor did he teach about the planetary essence types that Rodney Collin refers to in *The Theory of Celestial Influence*.

In *The Tales*, Gurdjieff writes about the ways in which three-brained beings "love" someone:

> ... or because his nose is much like the nose of that female or male, with whom thanks to the cosmic law of "polarity" or "type" a relation has been established which has not yet been broken ... [1]

He also writes:

> Love of consciousness evokes the same in response
> Love of feeling evokes the opposite
> Love of body depends only on type and polarity. [2]

However, he does not explain what he means here by type. In describing the "acting" of the Babylonian mysterists, he writes:

> Well then, these three learned beings who were thus cast impromptu by the fourth learned being for fulfilling every kind of perception and manifestation, which had to flow by law, of types foreign to them, or, as your favorites say, of 'strange roles,' ... [3]

He adds:

> ... because the learned beings of the planet Earth of that time were very well aware of what is called the 'law-of-typicality,' and that the three-brained beings of their planet

---

[1] *The Tales p358*
[2] *The Tales p361*
[3] *The Tales p848*

are ultimately formed into twenty-seven different definite types, ... [1]

Later, in discussing Judas, he provides a different count of types. He writes:

> when this Sacred Individual Jesus Christ, intentionally actualized from Above in a planetary body of a terrestrial being, completely formed Himself for a corresponding existence, He decided to actualize the mission imposed on Him from Above, through the way of enlightening the reason of these three-brained terrestrial beings, by means of twelve different types of beings, chosen from among them and who were specially enlightened and prepared by him personally.[2]

Towards the beginning of the final chapter of *The Tales*, "From The Author," he writes:

> I—or rather, this time, that dominant something in my common presence which now represents the sum of the results obtained from the data crystallized during my life, data which engender, among other things, in a man who has in general set himself the aim, so to say "to mentate actively impartially" during the process of responsible existence, the ability to penetrate and understand the psyche of people of various types ... [3]

And to add to that information, but not to lessen the confusion, in *The Herald of Coming Good*, he writes:

> ... I was compelled to give them all up and to undertake the organization of my own "circle" on quite new principles, with a staff of people chosen specially by me.
>
> I decided to do so mainly for the reason that, meeting then a great number of people usually composing such circles, I had elucidated and established the fact that in such societies foregather generally people of three or four definite "types", whereas it was necessary for me —in order to observe the manifestations of man's psyche in his waking state—to have at my disposal representatives of all the 28 "categories-of-

[1] *The Tales p486*
[2] *The Tales p740*
[3] *The Tales pp1186-1187*

types" existing on Earth, as they were established in ancient times.[1]

The 1931 Manuscript contains a further reference to "types" in the part that discusses astrologers. Gurdjieff writes:

... indicated just what they had to do to their own planetary body at which definite periods of the Krentonalnian movements of their planet—as for instance, in which direction to lie, how to breathe, which movements to make in preference, with which types to avoid relations and many things of the same kind.[2]

[1] The Herald of Coming Good, p19
[2] The 1931 Manuscript, p270

the esteemed Mullah Nassr Eddin characterizes by the words: "All they can do is to wrangle with pigs about the quality of oranges."

This kind of people among us who have been turned into, so to say, "moths" destroying the good prepared and left for us by our ancestors and by time, have not the slightest notion and have probably never even heard of the screamingly obvious fact that, during the preparatory age, there is acquired in the brain functioning of every creature, and of man also, a particular and definite property, the automatic actualization and manifestation of which the ancient Korkolans called the "law of association," and that the process of the mentation of every creature, especially man, flows exclusively in accordance with this law.

Wrangle with pigs

... that these languages are compiled by people, or rather "grammarians," who are in respect of knowledge of the given language exactly similar to those biped animals whom the esteemed Mullah Nassr Eddin characterizes by the words: "All they can do is to wrangle with pigs about the quality of oranges."

wrangle: late 14c., from Low German *wrangeln* "to dispute, to wrestle," related to Middle Low German *wringen*, from Proto-Germanic *wrang-*, from *wrengh-*, nasalized variant of *wergh-* "to turn." Meaning "take charge of horses" is by 1897, American English. The noun is recorded from 1540s.

pig: probably from Old English *picg*, found in compounds, further etymology unknown. Originally "young pig" (the word for adults was swine). Apparently related to Low German *bigge*, applied to persons, usually in contempt, since 1540s; the derogatory meaning "police officer" has been a pat of underworld slang at least since 1811. Sailors and fishermen are said to avoid uttering the word "pig" at sea, in case it should bring bad luck—a superstition perhaps based on the fate of the Gadarene swine, who drowned.

quality: c. 1300, "temperament, character, disposition," from Old French *qualite* "quality, nature, characteristic," from Latin *qualitatem*, "a quality, property; nature, state, condition" (said to have been coined by Cicero to translate Greek *poiotes*), from *qualis* "what kind of a." Meaning "degree of goodness" is late 14c. Meaning "social rank, position" is c. 1400.

The symbol "pig" is sometimes used to refer to man (derogatorily), as in the English saying:

Cats are superior, dogs are inferior, pigs are man's equal.

Also, in *Life Is Real Only Then, When 'I Am'*, Gurdjieff provides the following saying:

"A man is not a pig to forget good, nor is he a cat to remember evil."

While pigs can in general eat most kinds of food, citrus fruit can upset their stomachs and thus they are rarely fed such food. There is no sense in wrangling with pigs about the quality of food in which they have no genuine interest.

Moths

This kind of people among us who have been turned into, so to say, "moths" destroying the good prepared and left for us by our ancestors and by time, have not the slightest notion and have probably never even heard of the screamingly obvious fact that, ...

moth: Old English *moððe* (Northumbrian *mohðe*), Old Norse *motti*, Middle Dutch *motte*, Dutch *mot*, German *motte* all mean "moth." Perhaps related to Old English *maða*, "maggot." Until 16c. was used mostly to denote the larva and usually in reference to devouring clothes, which makes sense as it is only the larvae that devour clothes.

Gurdjieff will have known that "moth" is a New Testament symbol. It can be found in *The New Testament*: Matthew vi.19-20, as follows:

Lay not up for yourselves treasures upon earth, where moth and rust doth corrupt, and where thieves break through and steal:

But lay up for yourselves treasures in heaven, where neither moth nor rust doth corrupt, and where thieves do not break through nor steal.

Korkolans

He continues:

... during the preparatory age, there is acquired in the brain functioning of every creature, and of man also, a particular and definite property, the automatic actualization and manifestation of which the ancient Korkolans called the "law of association," and that the process of the mentation

of every creature, especially man, flows exclusively in accordance with this law.

The Korkolans that Gurdjieff refers to could be the Colchians (Kolkhians) as this is the most direct and compelling phonetic equivalent. The Colchians were the inhabitants of Colchis, an ancient kingdom on the coast of the Black Sea, centered in present-day western Georgia. Colchis was the famous destination of Jason and the Argonauts in their quest for the Golden Fleece.

Alternatively, it may be a reference to the ancient inhabitants of the Caucasus. The word "Caucasus" comes directly from the Ancient Greek word *Kaukasos* (Καύκασος). This word was claimed by the Roman historian Pliny the Elder, to be a Greek version of a Scythian word, *kroy-khasis*. In the Scythian language, this supposedly meant "ice-shining" or "white with snow," a fitting description for the high, snow-covered mountain range.

The assertion that "the process of the mentation of every creature, especially man, flows exclusively in accordance with" association, is worthy of pondering. Earlier in the text, referring to the Greek language, Gurdjieff writes:

> ... which I spoke in childhood and, as might be said, the "taste of the automatic associative power of which" I still retain.

According to Gurdjieff, languages are imbued with "automatic associative power."

In view of the fact that I have happened here accidentally to touch upon a question which has lately become one of my so to speak "hobbies," namely, the process of human mentation, I consider it possible, without waiting for the corresponding place predetermined by me for the elucidation of this question, to state already now in this first chapter at least something concerning that axiom which has accidentally become known to me, that on Earth in the past it has been usual in every century that every man, in whom there arises the boldness to attain the right to be considered by others and to consider himself a "conscious thinker," should be informed while still in the early years of his responsible existence that man has in general two kinds of mentation: one kind, mentation by thought, in which words, always possessing a relative sense, are employed; and the other kind, which is proper to all animals as well as to man, which I would call "mentation by form."

The second kind of mentation, that is, "mentation by form," by which, strictly speaking, the exact sense of all

CHAPTER IV

The Arousing of Thought 15-22

Gurdjieff puts a significant amount of effort into preparing the reader to read his book. It's clear that he knows the reader will miss most of what he is trying to convey on the first few readings of the book, even though it is there on the page. The diligent reader will, however, return again and again to the text knowing that they never fully understood the words on previous readings.

Eventually the reader will realize that they will need to know more about themselves just to read the book.

Hobbies

In view of the fact that I have happened here accidentally to touch upon a question which has lately become one of my so to speak "hobbies," namely, the process of human mentation, ...

hobby: 1400, *hobi*, "small, active horse," short for *hobyn* (mid-14c.; late 13c. in Anglo-Latin), probably originally a proper name for a horse (compare *dobbin*), a diminutive of Robert or Robin. The modern sense of "a favorite pursuit, object, or topic" is from 1816, a shortening of *hobbyhorse*. It was also used in the "morris horse" (morris dancing) sense (1760) and the "child's toy horse" sense (1680s).

The horse is a primary metaphor for the emotional center. Gurdjieff's use of the word could also be viewed as ironic.

He didn't happen upon this topic "accidentally" he leads us up to it as the previous paragraph clearly indicates.

Conscious thinker

> ... that on Earth in the past it has been usual in every century that every man, in whom there arises the boldness to attain the right to be considered by others and to consider himself a "conscious thinker," should be informed while still in the early years of his responsible existence that man has in general two kinds of mentation: ...

It is clearly an inexactitude to suggest that anything of the kind "has been usual." The phrase "in whom there arises the boldness to attain the right to be considered by others and to consider himself a 'conscious thinker,'" is curious.

It implies that "boldness" is required of those who wish to be a "conscious thinker." "Bold" means "brave, confident, strong," both in current usage and also etymologically. "Conscious thinker," is most likely wrapped in quotes to highlight the fact that "conscious thinking" is distinct from our normal thinking.

Mentation by thought

> ... one kind, mentation by thought, in which words, always possessing a relative sense, are employed; ...

Gurdjieff insists that there are two kinds of mentation. He chooses the word "mentation" rather than "thinking" for a reason. "Mentation" is an act of the mind whereas "mentation by thought" is an act led by the intellectual center, depending heavily on its use of words and their manipulation. This he signals in the phrase: "in which words, always possessing a relative sense, are employed."

We can reference *In Search of the Miraculous* by P D Ouspensky for a more complete description of mentation by thought. Ouspensky quotes Gurdjieff as saying:

> "The division of man into seven categories, or seven numbers, explains thousands of things which otherwise cannot be understood. This division gives the first conception of relativity as applied to man. Things may be one thing or another thing according to the kind of man

from whose point of view, or in relation to whom, they are taken.

"In accordance with this, all the inner and all the outer manifestations of man, all that belongs to man, and all that is created by him, is also divided into seven categories.

"It can now be said that there exists a knowledge number one, based upon imitation or upon instincts, or learned by heart, crammed or drilled into a man. Number one, if he is man number one in the full sense of the term, learns everything like a parrot or a monkey.

"The knowledge of man number two is merely the knowledge of what he likes; what he does not like he does not know. Always and in everything he wants something pleasant. Or, if he is a sick man, he will, on the contrary, know only what he dislikes, what repels him and what evokes in him fear, horror, and loathing.[1]

"The knowledge of man number three is knowledge based upon subjectively logical thinking, upon words, upon literal understanding. It is the knowledge of bookworms, of scholastics...

Gurdjieff then goes on to explain that the division into seven categories applies to everything relating to man.

"The same order of division into seven categories must be applied to everything relating to man. There is art number one, that is the art of man number one, imitative, copying art, or crudely primitive and sensuous art such as the dances and music of savage peoples. There is art number two, sentimental art; art number three, intellectual, invented art; and there must be art number four, number five, and so on.

"In exactly the same way there exists the religion of man number one, that is to say, a religion consisting of rites, of external forms, of sacrifices and ceremonies of imposing splendor and brilliance, or, on the contrary, of a gloomy, cruel, and savage character, and so on. There is the religion of man number two; the religion of faith, love, adoration, impulse, enthusiasm, which soon becomes transformed into

---

[1] *In Search of the Miraculous by P D Ouspensky, p72-73*

the religion of persecution, oppression, and extermination of 'heretics' and 'heathens.' There is the religion of man number three; the intellectual, theoretical religion of proofs and arguments, based upon logical deductions, considerations, and interpretations...[1]

Mentation by form

The second kind of mentation, that is, "mentation by form," by which, strictly speaking, the exact sense of all writing must be also perceived, and after conscious confrontation with information already possessed, be assimilated, ...

It is necessary to analyze the text in some detail in order to be certain of what Gurdjieff is trying to convey. We begin with the word "form."

form: c. 1200, *forme, fourme*, "semblance, image, likeness," from Old French *forme, fourme*, "physical form, appearance; pleasing looks; shape, image; way, manner" (12c.), from Latin *forma* "form, contour, figure, shape; appearance, looks; an outline, a model, pattern, design; sort, kind condition," a word of unknown prior origin. From c. 1300 as "physical shape (of something), contour, outline," of a person, "shape of the body;" also "appearance, likeness"; also "the imprint of an object." From c. 1300 as "correct or appropriate way of doing something; established procedure; traditional usage; formal etiquette." Mid-14c. as "instrument for shaping; a mould;" late 14c. as "way in which something is done," also "pattern of a manufactured object." Used widely from late 14c. in theology and Platonic philosophy with senses "archetype of a thing or class; the Platonic essence of a thing; the formative principle."

The meaning Gurdjieff is indicating appears closest to "Platonic essence of a thing; the formative principle." However, he is strongly asserting that within this mode of mentation each individual establishes (by habit) an entirely subjective inner meaning for every word.

[1] *In Search of the Miraculous* by P D Ouspensky, p73

The text, if read seriously, obliges the reader to consider their personal "mentation by form." Their mode of inner association that links sounds to inner images, not well defined words. The implication is that, in "mentation by form," an image is invoked in association with a word or collection of words, through sensation. He writes:

> Accordingly, in the brains of people of different races and conditions dwelling in different geographical localities, there are formed about one and the same thing or even idea, a number of quite independent forms, which during functioning, that is to say, association, evoke in their being some sensation or other which subjectively conditions a definite picturing, and which picturing is expressed by this, that, or the other word, that serves only for its outer subjective expression.

> That is why each word, for the same thing or idea, almost always acquires for people of different geographical locality and race a very definite and entirely different so to say "inner content."

For example, if we consider a common word like "house," any image that might arise in association with that word would be different for someone from Paris compared to someone from New York, and different again for someone who lived in rural France or rural America. The subjective associations to it would be different, arising from the experience of a house, which would vary by culture and geographic location and would include personal experience.

Clearly the difference in meaning of conceptual words, such as "justice" or "intelligence," would be equally as tainted, if not more so, by the personal and cultural context within which they were experienced and the habitual associations that were formed.

Gurdjieff asserts in the text that "mentation by form" is proper to all animals as well as to man. This must mean that "mentation by form" is primarily established by the emotional center and moving/instinctive centers.

As man has, additionally, an intellectual center, the subjective experiences of the emotional center and moving/instinctive centers, naturally taint any intellectual definition that a man might attach to a given word. While "mentation by thought" is possible for man alone, it does not develop naturally. Mentation by form develops from the moment of birth and is the normal foundation of human mentation.

Must be perceived…

the exact sense of all writing must be also perceived, and after conscious confrontation with information already possessed, be assimilated,…

Gurdjieff says that the exact sense of all writing must also be perceived using "mentation by form." This is not avoidable. This is the mentation that we have established since being born and which is completely automatic for us. If we wanted with all our heart not to experience writing in this way, we still could not avoid doing so.

confrontation: 1630s, "action of bringing two parties face to face," for examination and discovery of the truth, from Medieval Latin *confrontationem* (nominative *confront-atio*), noun of action from past-participle stem of *confrontari*, from assimilated form of Latin *com* "with, together" + *frontem* (nominative *frons*) "forehead."

assimilate: early 15c., in physiology, "absorb into and make part of the body," from Latin *assimilatus*, past participle of *assimilare*, *assimulare* "to make like, copy, imitate, assume the form of; feign, pretend," from assimilated form of *ad* "to" + *simulare* "make similar," from *similis* "like, resembling, of the same kind." Meaning "make alike, cause to resemble," and intransitive sense "become incorporated into" are from 1620s. In linguistics, "bring into accordance or agreement in speech," from 1854.

writing must be also perceived, and after conscious confrontation with information already possessed, be assimilated, is formed in people in dependence upon the conditions of geographical locality, climate, time, and, in general, upon the whole environment in which the arising of the given man has proceeded and in which his existence has flowed up to manhood.

"Accordingly, in the brains of people of different races and conditions dwelling in different geographical localities, there are formed about one and the same thing or even idea, a number of quite independent forms, which during functioning, that is to say, association, evoke in their being some sensation or other which subjectively conditions a definite picturing, and which picturing is expressed by this, that, or the other word, that serves only for its outer subjective expression.

That is why each word, for the same thing or idea, almost always acquires for people of different geographical locality and race a very definite and entirely different so to say "inner content."

In other words, if in the entirety of any man who has arisen and been formed in any locality, from the results of the specific local influences and impressions a certain "form" has been composed, and this form evokes in him by association the sensation of a definite "inner content," and consequently of a definite picturing or notion for the expression of which he employs one or another word which has eventually become habitual, and as I have said, subjective to him, then the hearer of that word, in whose being, owing to different conditions of his arising and growth, there has been formed concerning the given word a form of a different "inner content," will always perceive and of course infallibly understand that same word in quite another sense.

Different races and conditions

Accordingly, in the brains of people of different races and conditions dwelling in different geographical localities, there are formed about one and the same thing or even idea, a number of quite independent forms, which during functioning, that is to say, association, evoke in their being some sensation or other which subjectively conditions a definite picturing, and which is expressed by this, that, or the other word, that serves only for its outer subjective expression.

Gurdjieff talks about the consequences of the differences in the development of "mentation by form" in people with different upbringings, throwing more light on the process of mentation. He describes a chain of links from a thing or idea to a form, which evokes a sensation, conditioning a picturing, which is expressed by a word.

evoke: 1620s, from French *évoquer* or directly from Latin *evocare* "call out, rouse, summon," from assimilated form of *ex* "out" + *vocare* "to call." Often more or less with a sense of "calling spirits," or being called by them. Of feelings, memories, etc., by 1856.

condition: late 15c., "to make conditions, stipulate," from *condition* (n.). Meaning "subject to something as a condition" is from 1520s; sense of "form a prerequisite of" is from 1868. Meaning "to bring to a desired condition" is from 1844; psychological sense of "teach or accustom (a person or animal) to certain habits or responses" is from 1909.

Gurdjieff restates the problem surrounding the objective understanding of words. Breaking his words up, a little:

- *In other words, if in the entirety of any man who has arisen and been formed in any locality, from the results of the specific local influences and impressions*

- *a certain "form" has been composed,*

- *and this form evokes in him by association the sensation of a definite "inner content,"*

- and consequently of a definite picturing or notion for the expression of which he employs one or another word which has eventually become habitual, and as I have said, subjective to him,

- then the hearer of that word, in whose being, owing to different conditions of his arising and growth, there has been formed concerning the given word a form of a different "inner content,"

- will always perceive and of course infallibly understand that same word in quite another sense.

This fact, by the way, can with attentive and impartial observation be very clearly established when one is present at an exchange of opinions between persons belonging to two different races or who arose and were formed in different geographical localities.

And so, cheerful and swaggering candidate for a buyer of my wiseacrings, having warned you that I am going to write not as "professional writers" usually write but quite otherwise, I advise you, before embarking on the reading of my further expositions, to reflect seriously and only then to undertake it. If not, I am afraid for your hearing and other perceptive and also digestive organs which may be already so thoroughly automatized to the "literary language of the intelligentsia" existing in the present period of time on Earth, that the reading of these writings of mine might affect you very, very cacophonously, and from this you might lose your ... you know what? ... your appetite for your favorite dish and for your psychic specificness which particularly titillates your "inside" and which proceeds in you on seeing your neighbor, the brunette.

For such a possibility, ensuing from my language, or rather, strictly speaking, from the form of my mentation, I am, thanks to oft-repeated past experiences, already quite as convinced with my whole being as a "thoroughbred donkey" is convinced of the right and justice of his obstinacy.

Now that I have warned you of what is most important, I am already tranquil about everything further. Even if any misunderstanding should arise on account of my writings, you alone will be entirely to blame, and my conscience will be as clear as for instance ... the ex-Kaiser Wilhelm's.

In all probability you are now thinking that I am, of course, a young man with an auspicious exterior and, as some express it, a "suspicious interior," and that, as a

The language of the intelligentsia

> If not, I am afraid for your hearing and other perceptive and also digestive organs which may be already so thoroughly automatized to the "literary language of the intelligentsia" existing in the present period of time on Earth, ...

Intelligentsia: "the intellectual class collectively," a loan word from Russian *intelligyentsiya*, c 1905, from Latin *intelligentia* "intelligence."

Naturally it is the intelligentsia, being the section of society from which most authors are drawn, that moulds the literary language of the day.

Gurdjieff warns us yet again that he will not write as "professional writers" usually write, and advises us to reflect seriously before reading any further.

The possible impact of the book

> ... that the reading of these writings of mine might affect you very, very cacophonously, and from this you might lose your ... you know what? ... your appetite for your favorite dish and for your psychic specificness which particularly titillates your "inside" and which proceeds in you on seeing your neighbor, the brunette.

Gurdjieff warns us that his writings will have an impact and may possibly have an impact that we perhaps wouldn't welcome, such as losing our physical or sexual appetite.

cacophony: (n.) 1650s, "harsh or unpleasant sound," probably via French *cacophonie* (16c.), from a Latinized form of Greek *kakophonia*, from *kakophonos* "harsh sounding," from *kakos* "bad, evil." Meaning "discordant sounds in music" is from 1789.

He doesn't say that his writing is cacophonous, but that its effect on you might be.

A thoroughbred donkey

For such a possibility, ensuing from my language, or rather, strictly speaking, from the form of my mentation, I am, thanks to oft-repeated past experiences, already quite as convinced with my whole being as a "thoroughbred donkey" is convinced of the right and justice of his obstinacy.

"Thoroughbred donkey" is a comical oxymoron, as becomes clear from the etymology of the two words.

thoroughbred: The earliest meaning, 1701, applied to persons, "thoroughly accomplished," from *thorough* + *bred*, the past tense of breed. In reference to horses, "of pure breed or stock," is from 1796; the noun is first recorded 1842. Thoroughbred refers specifically to the distinct breed of horse developed in England for the purpose of racing.

donkey: The familiar term for an ass, 1785, also *donky*, *donkie*, originally slang or dialectal, of uncertain origin. Perhaps a diminutive from dun "dull gray-brown." Donkeys are notoriously stubborn, so the word began to be applied to stupid, obstinate, or wrong-headed persons by 1840.

While there are purely bred donkeys, they would never be described as thoroughbred.

However, Gurdjieff's conviction might well be appropriately described by such an adjective.

Ex-Kaiser Wilhelm

Now that I have warned you of what is most important, I am already tranquil about everything further. Even if any misunderstanding should arise on account of my writings, you alone will be entirely to blame, and my conscience will be as clear as for instance ... the ex-Kaiser Wilhelm's.

Ex-Kaiser Wilhelm was the last German Emperor (Kaiser) and King of Prussia. He assumed the throne in 1888, subsequently launching Germany on a warlike course,

Fig 4. Kaiser Wilhelm II

eventually resulting in the outbreak of World War I. He gave German backing to Austria-Hungary in its war against Serbia, that followed from the assassination of Austria's Archduke Ferdinand.

After Germany's defeat in 1918, Wilhelm lost the support of the German army, abdicated and fled into exile in the Netherlands, where he died in 1941, during World War II.

Ex-Kaiser Wilhelm's conscience was anything but clear.

Auspicious and suspicious

After this passage, Gurdjieff goes on to talk about his motive for writing:

In all probability you are now thinking that I am, of course, a young man with an auspicious exterior and, as some express it, a "suspicious interior," and that, as a novice in writing, I am evidently intentionally being eccentric in the hope of becoming famous and thereby rich.

auspicious: 1590s, "of good omen," from Latin *auspicium* "divination by observing the flight of birds," from *auspex* (genitive *auspicis*) + *-ous*.

suspicious: (adj.) mid-14c., "deserving of or exciting suspicion," from Old French *sospecious*, from Latin *suspiciosus,* or *suspitiosus* "exciting suspicion, causing mistrust," also "full of suspicion, ready to suspect," from stem of *suspicere* "look up at." Meaning "full of suspicion, inclined to suspect in English is attested from c. 1400.

novice in writing, I am evidently intentionally being eccentric in the hope of becoming famous and thereby rich. If you indeed think so, then you are very, very mistaken. First of all, I am not young; I have already lived so much that I have been in my life, as it is said, "not only through the mill but through all the grindstones"; and secondly, I am in general not writing so as to make a career for myself, or so as to plant myself, as is said, "firm-footedly," thanks to this profession, which, I must add, in my opinion provides many openings to become a candidate d-i-r-e-c-t for "Hell"—assuming of course that such people can in general by their Being, perfect themselves even to that extent, for the reason that knowing nothing whatsoever themselves, they write all kinds of "claptrap" and thereby automatically acquiring authority, they become almost one of the chief factors, the totality of which steadily continues year by year, still further to diminish the, without this, already extremely diminished psyche of people.

And as regards my personal career, then thanks to all forces high and low and, if you like, even right and left, I have actualized it long ago, and have already long been standing on "firm feet" and even maybe on very good feet, and I moreover am certain that their strength is sufficient for many more years, in spite of all my past, present, and future enemies.

Yes, I think you might as well be told also about an idea which has only just arisen in my madcap brain, and namely, specially to request the printer, to whom I shall give my first book, to print this first chapter of my writings in such a way that anybody may read it before cutting the pages of the book itself, whereupon, on learning that it is not written in the usual manner, that is to say, for helping to produce in one's mentation, very smoothly and easily, exciting images and lulling reveries, he may, if he wishes,

I am not young

First of all, I am not young; I have already lived so much that I have been in my life, as it is said, "not only through the mill but through all the grindstones";

In reality almost everyone who buys this book knows that the author is no longer alive and is probably aware that the book wasn't published until after his death. The writing here is thus theatrical, a denial that the author is seeking fame and wealth through the adoption of an unusual literary style.

The phrase "not only through the mill but through all the grindstones" may derive from 2nd century Greek philosopher Sextus Empiricus, who wrote, "The millstones of the gods grind late, but they grind fine."

D-i-r-e-c-t

... and secondly, I am in general not writing so as to make a career for myself, or so as to plant myself, as is said, "firm-footedly," thanks to this profession, which, I must add, in my opinion provides many openings to become a candidate d-i-r-e-c-t for "Hell."

Gurdjieff's distinctive use of dashes between every letter of a word is a stylistic choice that can be taken to indicate extreme emphasis. It visually represents someone spelling the word out letter-by-letter as a parent might when teaching a child, trying to be precise.

Acquiring authority

... they write all kinds of "claptrap" and thereby auto-matically acquiring authority, they become almost one of the chief factors, the totality of which steadily continues year by year, still further to diminish the, without this, already extremely diminished psyche of people.

claptrap: 1730, "a trick to 'catch' applause," a stage term; from *clap* + *trap* (n.). Extended sense of "cheap, showy language" is from 1819; hence "nonsense, rubbish."

Gurdjieff's phrase "till further to diminish the, without this, already extremely diminished psyche of people" is a kind of refrain that occurs elsewhere in *The Tales*, indicating that although already weak, the psyche of man continues to get weaker because of his behaviour.

"Firm feet"

And as regards my personal career, then thanks to all forces high and low and, if you like, even right and left, I have actualized it long ago, and have already long been standing on "firm feet" and even maybe on very good feet, and I moreover am certain that their strength is sufficient for many more years, in spite of all my past, present, and future enemies.

He uses the term "firm-footedly" earlier and "firm feet" in this paragraph. It could be taken to mean "firm or secure financial position," although the intended meaning may go deeper, because Gurdjieff uses these directions: high, low, left and right. These are reminiscent of the Christian ritual of making the sign of the cross.

So we may also wonder if the use of "firm feet" in this context might relate to Christianity, since the words are wrapped in quotes. If so, then it may relate to a passage from Ephesians 6: 13-16 (particularly verse 15).

13 *Wherefore take unto you the whole armour of God, that ye may be able to withstand in the evil day, and having done all, to stand.*

14 *Stand therefore, having your loins girt about with truth, and having on the breastplate of righteousness;*

15 *And your feet shod with the preparation of the gospel of peace;*

16 *Above all, taking the shield of faith, wherewith ye shall be able to quench all the fiery darts of the wicked.*

Madcap[1]

Yes, I think you might as well be told also about an idea which has only just arisen in my madcap brain,

madcap: 1580s, noun ("person who acts madly or wildly") and adjective ("wild, harum-scarum"), from mad + cap, used figuratively for "head." The "cap" part is an old (obsolete in any other use) word meaning "head." So a "madcap" was originally a "mad-head," someone who "has bats in their belfry."

Gurdjieff continues to be self-deprecating. In this "preface" in addition to dispensing knowledge, he is partly arrogant, partly insulting to the reader and partly self-critical.

Cutting the pages of the book

... in such a way that anybody may read it before cutting the pages of the book itself ...

The practice of publishing books with unopened (or uncut) pages was common up until the early 20th century. The practice of selling books in this format dates back to the earliest printed books where pages were printed on large sheets, folded into groups of pages, and then lightly bound. Before the 19th century, books were often sold in temporary bindings expecting the buyer to take the book to a professional binder to have a permanent, custom binding created.

The practice remained common even as publishers began supplying books in "publisher's cloth" bindings (starting around the 1820s). Books from the 18th and 19th centuries are very frequently found with unopened pages, as the reader was still expected to use a paper knife (or letter opener) to slice open the folds as they read. It was a mark of a new, unread book.

With the rise of mass-market edition binding and the introduction of mechanical trimming methods like the guillotine cutter it became cheaper and faster for publishers to trim all the edges of the book block smooth and flush before

---

[1] *Gurdjieff names a comet Sakoor "madcap"—The Tales p56.*

binding. This gradually ended the common practice for most commercial books.

So the practice largely disappeared for mainstream publications by around 1900 to the 1930s in the US and UK. Nevertheless, it persisted longer for fine/limited editions and for books in some European countries, notably France.

... specially to request the printer, to whom I shall give my first book, to print this first chapter of my writings in such a way that anybody may read it before cutting the pages of the book itself ...

Again, this is theater rather than a feasible idea, as it involves a unique publishing process—trimming some of the pages of a book, but not others. And, of course, no volumes of *The Tales* were published in this way. It would additionally have required booksellers to co-operate and most likely they would not have done so.

Lulling reveries

... exciting images and lulling reveries, ...

lull: (v.) early 14c., *lullen* "to calm or hush to sleep," probably imitative of lu-lu sound used to lull a child to sleep (compare Swedish *lulla* "to hum a lullaby," German *lullen* "to rock," Middle Dutch *lollen* "to mutter"). Figurative use from 1570s; specifically "to quiet (suspicion) so as to delude into a sense of security" is from c. 1600.

reverie: (n.) mid-14c., *reuerye*, "wild conduct, frolic," from Old French *reverie*, *resverie* "revelry, raving, delirium" (Modern French *rêverie*), from *resver* "to dream, wander, rave" (12c., Modern French *rêver*), of uncertain origin. Meaning "daydream" is first attested 1650s, a reborrowing from French. As a type of musical composition, it is attested from 1880.

Gurdjieff emphasizes again that the book "is not written in the usual manner, for helping to produce in one's mentation, very smoothly and easily, exciting images and lulling reveries."

without wasting words with the bookseller, return it and get his money back, money perhaps earned by the sweat of his own brow.

I shall do this without fail, moreover, because I just now again remember the story of what happened to a Transcaucasian Kurd, which story I heard in my quite early youth and which in subsequent years, whenever I recalled it in corresponding cases, engendered in me an enduring and inextinguishable impulse of tenderness. I think it will be very useful for me, and also for you, if I relate this story to you somewhat in detail.

It will be useful chiefly because I have decided already to make the "salt," or as contemporary pureblooded Jewish businessmen would say, the "Tzimus" of this story, one of the basic principles of that new literary form which I intend to employ for the attainment of the aim I am now pursuing by means of this new profession of mine.

This Transcaucasian Kurd once set out from his village on some business or other to town, and there in the market he saw in a fruiterer's shop a handsomely arranged display of all kinds of fruit.

In this display, he noticed one "fruit," very beautiful in both color and form, and its appearance so took his fancy and he so longed to try it, that in spite of his having scarcely any money, he decided to buy without fail at least one of these gifts of Great Nature, and taste it.

Then, with intense eagerness, and with a courage not customary to him, he entered the shop and pointing with his horny finger to the "fruit" which had taken his fancy he asked the shopkeeper its price. The shopkeeper replied that a pound of the "fruit" would cost two cents.

Finding that the price was not at all high for what in his opinion was such a beautiful fruit, our Kurd decided to buy a whole pound.

Transcaucasian

Transcaucasia lies to south of the Caucasus Mountains, spanning the countries of Georgia, Azerbaijan and Armenia. To the north is Russia, to the east the Caspian Sea, and to the south Iran and Turkey. Kurdistan, the homeland of the Kurds, encircles Lake Van and the region south of Lake Urmia. Thus it spans a sizeable mountainous area south of Transcaucasia, which is primarily part of Turkey, but also northern Iraq and western Iran.

The word "Transcaucasia" is a Latin rendering of the Russian-language word "Zakavkazie," meaning (from the Russian perspective) "the area beyond the Caucasus Mountains." Historically, some Kurds have made their home in Transcaucasia. According to the latest available Armenian Census (2011), 37,470 Kurds were living in Armenia.

However, nowadays, the word "Caucasian" is frequently used to denote people who are 'white, or of European origin,' especially in America. The word literally means "from or related to the Caucasus Mountains."

The confusion of meaning that this word creates has a historical origin. The term was popularized in the context of racial classification by German anthropologist Johann Friedrich Blumenbach in the late 18th century (in his 1795 treatise *On the Natural Variety of Mankind*).

Blumenbach proposed a five-race taxonomy of humanity, placing the Caucasian group as the "highest." He chose the term because he believed the Caucasus region (particularly Georgia, whose people's skulls he studied) was the original cradle of humanity and represented the most beautiful and ideal form of mankind. Despite its clear racial bias, Blumenbach's taxonomy was highly influential, and consequently the term "Caucasian" became entrenched in various legal, governmental, and pseudo-scientific systems, particularly in the United States, as a synonym for people of European descent or "white people."

It is possible that Gurdjieff is using the word "Transcaucasian, "not to denote inhabitants of the geographical area, but as a metaphor for Europeans and Americans.

Kurd

We may want to consider why Gurdjieff chose the word (or racial description) "Kurd." The current population of Transcaucasia is roughly 16.9 million (Armenians, Georgians and Azerbaijanis) and only a small fraction of them are Kurds (about 53,000 or 3.1 percent)

However, the word derives from the Sumerian word, *karda*, which means "mountain." This makes sense because the Kurds' homeland is mountainous. The Kurds were nomadic.

So Gurdjieff may be choosing the word "Kurd" symbolically. The New Testament uses the term "mountain" (as for example, the Sermon on the Mount) to indicate a high level. Mountain dwellers can be thought of as those attracted to the higher, i.e. those who may be attracted to the Work.

So the Transcaucasian Kurd could suggest Europeans and Americans attracted to spiritual pursuits.

This may explain Gurdjieff's statement about his tale:

> ... in subsequent years, whenever I recalled it in corresponding cases, engendered in me an enduring and inextinguishable impulse of tenderness.

Tzimus and salt

> I have decided already to make the "salt," or as contemporary pureblooded Jewish businessmen would say, the "Tzimus" of this story, ...

Most likely, Gurdjieff borrowed "Tzimus" from Russian. Marvin Grossman, in an article published by the *Gurdjieff International Review*, dealt with it at length, concluding that it is Russian slang, means pith or essence, and is a word favored by Russian Jews.

This word has created a little confusion, because it sounds and looks suspiciously like the word "tsimmes" or "tzimmes," which is a Yiddish word for an Ashkenazi (German /East European Jewish) stewed dish made variously of carrots, prunes and sometimes meat.

However, Gurdjieff seems to indicate that the words "Tzimus" and "salt" have very similar meanings, as do "pith" and "salt."

According to Brian Simmons in *The Passion Translation New Testament (2nd Edition)*: "Rabbinical literature equates salt with wisdom." Salt is a preservative and in alchemy, it symbolizes 'that which survives the fire.'

New literary form

... one of the basic principles of that new literary form which I intend to employ for the attainment of the aim I am now pursuing by means of this new profession of mine

Gurdjieff does not say what this basic principle is so we can only guess what he means. One of the principles may be to use allegory (as the story of the Transcaucasian Kurd is obviously allegorical). Alternatively he may be referring to The New Testament symbolism which he employs in this story.

Town and village, town and country

This Transcaucasian Kurd once set out from his village on some business or other to town, and there in the market he saw in a fruiterer's shop a handsomely arranged display of all kinds of fruit.

There is a definite contrast in the text between a village and a town. Historically and etymologically, the word "village" (late 14c.) meant "inhabited place larger than a hamlet, but smaller than a town." By contrast, the word "town" indicates a large settlement, possibly fortified. Towns usually have markets whereas villages do not.

We can think of the village as indicative more of essence and the town, with its market and industry, as indicative of personality.

market: early 12c., "a meeting at a fixed time for buying and selling livestock and provisions, an occasion on which goods are publicly exposed for sale and buyers assemble to purchase," from Old North French *market* "marketplace, trade, commerce" (Old French *marchiet*, Modern French marché), from Latin *mercatus* "trading, buying and selling."

Gurdjieff uses the symbols of "town" and "market" on the one hand and "town" and "country(side)" on the other to represent personality and essence, both here and elsewhere in *The Tales*.

The town represents life in the Fourth Way sense of the place to apply the Work. The Kurd, who is primarily of essence (the countryside), goes into town and into the market and sees a fruit that he would only encounter in a market and is attracted to it.

Fruit

In this display, he noticed one "fruit," very beautiful in both color and form, and its appearance so took his fancy and he so longed to try it, that in spite of his having scarcely any money, he decided to buy without fail at least one of these gifts of Great Nature, and taste it.

We note that "fruit" is wrapped in quotes.

fruit: late 12c., "any vegetable product useful to humans or animals," from Old French *fruit* "fruit, fruit eaten as dessert; harvest; virtuous action" (12c.), from Latin *fructus* "an enjoyment, delight, satisfaction; proceeds, produce, fruit, crops," from *frug-*, stem of *frui* "to use, enjoy," from suffixed form of PIE root *bhrug-* "to enjoy," with derivatives referring to agricultural products. Meaning "offspring, progeny, child" is from mid-13c.; that of "any consequence, outcome, or result" is from late 14c. Meaning "odd person, eccentric" is from 1910; that of "male homosexual" is from 1935, underworld slang. Fruit salad recorded from 1861; fruit-cocktail from 1900; fruit-bat by 1869.

Symbolically, fruit is the produce of man (New Testament: "by their fruit ye shall know them"). So possibly this is the produce of real man. And in the context of *The Tales* we would be inclined to believe that.

Fancy

fancy: mid-15c., *fantsy* "inclination, liking," contraction of fantasy. It took the older and longer word's sense of "inclination, whim, desire." Meaning "the productive imagination" is from 1580s. That of "a fanciful image or conception" is from 1660s. Meaning "fans of an amusement or sport, collectively" is attested by 1735, especially (though not originally) of the prize ring. The adjective is recorded from 1751 in the sense "fine, elegant, ornamental" (as opposed to plain); later as "involving fancy, of a fanciful nature" (1800). Fancy man attested by 1811.

The word "fancy" is used repeatedly later in *The Tales* when Beelzebub speaks to Hassein. He refers many times to the three-brained beings who have taken Hassein's fancy.

Scarcely any money

... in spite of his having scarcely any money ...

Money is used to symbolize energy at several points throughout *The Tales*. Additionally those in the Work can be regarded as poor in the New Testament sense of the word.

Taste

taste: c. 1300, "to touch, to handle," from Old French *taster* "to taste, sample by mouth; enjoy" (13c.), earlier "to feel, touch, pat, stroke" (12c., Modern French *tâter*), from Vulgar Latin *tastare*, apparently an alteration (perhaps by influence of *gustare*) of *taxtare*, a frequentative form of Latin *taxare* "evaluate, handle." Meaning "to take a little food or drink" is from c. 1300; that of "to perceive by sense of taste" is recorded from mid-14c.

In order to experience the "fruit" it must inevitably be tasted.

Gifts of Great Nature

Gurdjieff introduces the idea that fruits are a gift of nature. The reader may have thought of fruit as the means that various plants and trees continue their species rather than as a gift of nature. He also introduces the concept of Great Nature here, for the first time.

Courage

Then, with intense eagerness, and with a courage not customary to him, he entered the shop ...

courage: c. 1300, *corage*, "heart (as the seat of emotions)," hence "spirit, temperament, state or frame of mind," from Old French *corage* "heart, innermost feelings; temper" (12c., Modern French courage), from Vulgar Latin *coraticum*, from Latin *cor* "heart." Meaning "valor, quality of mind which enables one to meet danger and trouble without fear" is from late 14c. In this sense, Old English had *ellen*, which also meant "zeal, strength." Words for "heart" are also common metaphors for inner strength. In Middle English, the word was used broadly for "what is in one's mind or thoughts," hence "bravery," but also "wrath, pride, confidence, lustiness," or any sort of inclination, and it was used in various phrases, such as *bold corage* "brave heart," *careful corage* "sad heart," *fre corage* "free will," *wikked corage* "evil heart."

Unless the Kurd had a morbid fear of shops, it's unlikely that he would need courage to enter a shop and buy something. The courage must thus refer to his intention to do something new and unfamiliar. A similar kind of courage is found in those who dare to engage with The Work.

Horny finger

and pointing with his horny finger to the "fruit" which had taken his fancy he asked the shopkeeper its price.

Fingers are not usually described as horny. If you look up the etymology of "horny," it originally refers to horns on the head.

horny: late 14c., "made of horn," from *horn* (n.) + *-y*. From 1690s as "callous, resembling horn." The colloquial meaning "lustful, sexually aroused," was in use by 1889, and is now the usual meaning of the word. Horn as a noun was once also a popular name for a domestic cow.

callous: c. 1400, "hardened," in the physical sense, from Latin *callosus* "thick-skinned," from *callus, callum* "hard skin". The figurative sense of "unfeeling, hardened in the mind" was in English by 1670s.

Horns are used much later in *The Tales* to symbolize degrees of Reason (the higher degrees being indicated by more tines); Beelzebub's Reason at the end of *The Tales* is measured by the way that his horns grow.

So the "horny finger" may imply "a wise finger."

Cents and pound

The shopkeeper replied that a pound of the "fruit" would cost two cents.

Finding that the price was not at all high for what in his opinion was such a beautiful fruit, our Kurd decided to buy a whole pound.

Note that here we depart from what would be the local currency in Transcaucasia (cents are not used in any of the countries of Transcaucasia) and from local units of weight (pounds are not used in any of the countries). The story adopts American currency and units of weight.

Having finished his business in town, he set off again on foot for home the same day.

Walking at sunset over the hills and dales, and willy-nilly perceiving the exterior visibility of those enchanting parts of the bosom of Great Nature, the Common Mother, and involuntarily inhaling a pure air uncontaminated by the usual exhalations of industrial towns, our Kurd quite naturally suddenly felt a wish to gratify himself with some ordinary food also; so sitting down by the side of the road, he took from his provision bag some bread and the "fruit" he had bought which had looked so good to him, and leisurely began to eat.

But ... horror of horrors! ... very soon everything inside him began to burn. But in spite of this he kept on eating.

And this hapless biped creature of our planet kept on eating, thanks only to that particular human inherency which I mentioned at first, the principle of which I intended, when I decided to use it as the foundation of the new literary form I have created, to make, as it were, a "guiding beacon" leading me to one of my aims in view, and the sense and meaning of which moreover you will, I am sure, soon grasp—of course according to the degree of your comprehension—during the reading of any subsequent chapter of my writings, if, of course, you take the risk and read further, or, it may perhaps be that even at the end of this first chapter you will already "smell" something.

And so, just at the moment when our Kurd was overwhelmed by all the unusual sensations proceeding within him from this strange repast on the bosom of Nature, there came along the same road a fellow villager of his, one reputed by those who knew him to be very clever and experienced; and, seeing that the whole face of the Kurd was aflame, that his eyes were streaming with tears, and

At sunset

Walking at sunset over the hills and dales, ...

When, in *The Tales*, Gurdjieff refers to night and day, usually he's not referring to literal night and day, but metaphorically to waking sleep (night) and to consciousness (day). So sunset is the borderland between the two.

Willy-nilly

...and willy-nilly perceiving the exterior visibility of those enchanting parts of the bosom of Great Nature, the Common Mother, and involuntarily inhaling a pure air uncontaminated by the usual exhalations of industrial towns, our Kurd quite naturally suddenly felt a wish to gratify himself with some ordinary food also;

willy-nilly: c. 1600, contraction of "will I, nill I," or "will he, nill he," or "will ye, nill ye," literally "with or without the will of the person concerned."

The Kurd cannot help but perceive the beauty of nature as he walks back to his village. Here, Gurdjieff refers to the bosom of Great Nature, the Common Mother, emphasizing the fact that nature can directly feed us nourishing, beautiful impressions.

Bread

...so sitting down by the side of the road, he took from his provision bag some bread and the "fruit" he had bought which had looked so good to him, and leisurely began to eat.

Bread is another Biblical symbol indicating knowledge (bread of heaven, Christ feeding the crowd with two fish and five loaves of bread, Christ tempted by the devil to turn stones into bread, bread as the flesh of Christ, etc.). He eats bread with the "fruit." He invokes his spirit.

"Provision bag" is an odd choice of words. "Provision" indicates what is prepared for the future. So, metaphorically, *The Tales* (the fruit) is in our provision bag. He leisurely begins to eat the bread and the fruit.

Horror of horrors

But ... horror of horrors! ...

horror: early 14c., "feeling of disgust;" late 14c., "emotion of horror or dread," also "thing which excites horror," from Old French *horror* (12c., Modern French *horreur*) and directly from Latin *horror* "horror, dread, veneration, religious awe," a figurative use, literally "a shaking, trembling (as with cold or fear), shudder, chill," from *horrere* "to bristle with fear, shudder."

He starts to eat the red peppers and "horror of horrors"— religious awe of religious awe?

Burning inside

... very soon everything inside him began to burn.

Hot red peppers will certainly burn your mouth, but they will not burn you inside. But reading *The Tales* may well set fire to your inner world.

Hapless

But in spite of this he kept on eating.

And this hapless biped creature of our planet kept on eating, thanks only to that particular human inherency which I mentioned at first, the principle of which I intended, when I decided to use it as the foundation of the new literary form I have created

The choice of the words "hapless" and "biped" is curious. "Hapless" could simply be taken to mean unlucky, although there is nothing in the story of the Kurd to indicate that his purchase was unlucky. One might in fact form the opposite opinion.

The etymology of "hap" is:

hap: c. 1200, "chance, a person's luck, fortune, fate;" also "unforeseen occurrence," from Old Norse *happ* "chance, good luck," from Proto-Germanic *hap-* (source of Old English *gehæp* "convenient, fit"). Meaning "good fortune" in English is from early 13c. The word seems only to have had positive connotations in Old Norse.

In this context, someone who is "hapless" might be someone who is not directly under the law of accident—laws of chance—but is instead influenced by the laws of fate.

The word "biped," meaning two-footed, may refer to the Christian symbol of the foot as the point at which you interact with life. The left foot indicates essence and the right personality. Thus "hapless biped" might, metaphorically, indicate someone who is attracted to the Work.

Gurdjieff makes it clear that he is challenging the reader to dare to read the book. He emphasizes that it will be difficult, and that the difficulty he has created is a "guiding beacon" of his new literary form. Anyone who has struggled with *The Tales* knows full well that it is an entirely new literary form.

Repast

> And so, just at the moment when our Kurd was overwhelmed by all the unusual sensations proceeding within him from this strange repast on the bosom of Nature, ...

repast: late 14c., from Old French *repast* (Modern French *repas*) "a meal, food," from Late Latin *repastus* "meal" (also source of Spanish *repasto*, noun use of past participle of *repascere* "to feed again," from Latin *re-* "repeatedly" (see *re-*) + *pascere* "to graze," from PIE root *pa-* "to feed." The verb (intransitive) is from late 15c.

The etymology of "repast" implies "feeding again" on the bosom of Nature.

Aflame and eyes streaming

> and, seeing that the whole face of the Kurd was aflame, that his eyes were streaming with tears, and that in spite of this, as if intent upon the fulfillment of his most important duty, he was eating real "red pepper pods," he said to him:

Again the physical details do not align exactly with the experience of eating hot peppers. The capsaicin in hot peppers binds to pain receptors in the mouth, tricking the nervous system into thinking your body is overheating. Tears and sweating may also occur, but streaming with tears is an exaggeration. However the experience of remorse may provoke tears and fire in the inner world.

In a Paris meeting on December 7, 1941, Gurdjieff said:

> One needs fire. Without fire, there will never be anything. This fire is suffering, intentional suffering, without which it is impossible to create anything. One must prepare, must know what will make one suffer and when it is there, make use of it. Only you can prepare, only you know what makes you suffer, makes the fire which cooks, cements, crystallizes, does.

> Suffer by your defects, in your pride, in your egoism. Remind yourself of the aim. Without prepared suffering there is nothing, for by as much as one is conscious, there is no more suffering. No further process, nothing. That is why with your conscience you must prepare what is necessary. You owe to nature. The food you eat which nourishes your life. You must pay for these cosmic substances. You have a duty, an obligation, to repay by conscious work.

that in spite of this, as if intent upon the fulfillment of his most important duty, he was eating real "red pepper pods," he said to him:

"What are you doing, you Jericho jackass? You'll be burnt alive! Stop eating that extraordinary product, so unaccustomed for your nature."

But our Kurd replied: "No, for nothing on Earth will I stop. Didn't I pay my last two cents for them? Even if my soul departs from my body I shall still go on eating."

Whereupon our resolute Kurd—it must of course be assumed that he was such—did not stop, but continued eating the "red pepper pods."

After what you have just perceived, I hope there may already be arising in your mentation a corresponding mental association which should, as a result, effectuate in you, as it sometimes happens to contemporary people, that which you call, in general, understanding, and that in the present case you will understand just why I, well knowing and having many a time commiserated with this human inherency, the inevitable manifestation of which is that if anybody pays money for something, he is bound to use it to the end, was animated in the whole of my entirety with the idea, arisen in my mentation, to take every possible measure in order that you, as is said "my brother in appetite and in spirit"—in the event of your proving to be already accustomed to reading books, though of all kinds, yet nevertheless only those written exclusively in the aforesaid "language of the intelligentsia"—having already paid money for my writings and learning only afterwards that they are not written in the usual convenient and easily read language, should not be compelled as a consequence of the said human inherency, to read my writings through to the end at all costs, as our poor Transcaucasian Kurd was compelled to go on with his eating of what he had

The Jericho jackass

he said to him:

"What are you doing, you Jericho jackass? You'll be burnt alive! Stop eating that extraordinary product, so unaccustomed for your nature."

The fellow villager is reputed to be clever and experienced—he recognizes that the Kurd is eating, "as if intent upon fulfillment of his most important duty." And yet, he tells him to stop—perhaps because he is acting against his nature.

It is not our nature that requires us to work on ourselves, to develop Will. We satisfy the needs of Nature mechanically by our physical processes. The Kurd, however, chooses struggle, and perhaps that is our most important duty.

A jackass is a male donkey. Christ came from Jericho to Jerusalem for his trial and crucifixion. Outside Jerusalem, he mounted a male donkey, a jackass. The Jericho jackass is an alliterative phrase that hints at this. By eating the red peppers, then, you may become the vehicle that carries the Christ within you towards the crucifixion.

Our Kurd

But our Kurd replied:

Here, Gurdjieff refers to the Kurd as "our Kurd" and later on the page as "our poor Transcaucasian Kurd," suggesting that the Kurd is a part of us.

The last two cents

But our Kurd replied: "No, for nothing on Earth will I stop. Didn't I pay my last two cents for them? Even if my soul departs from my body I shall still go on eating."

For nothing on earth would he stop eating - "for nothing on earth," possibly because there's "nothing on earth" he cares deeply about. The 'two cents' probably refers to the widow's mites passage in *The New Testament, Mark 12:42-44.* A mite was a small coin, sometimes translated as a cent:

And there came a certain poor widow, and she threw in two mites, which make a farthing. And he called unto him his disciples, and saith unto them, Verily I say unto you, That this poor widow hath cast more in, than all they which have cast into the treasury: For all they did cast in of their abundance; but she of her want did cast in all that she had, even all her living.

It is only at this point that the two cents are referred to as the "last two cents."

fancied for its appearance alone—that "not to be joked with" noble red pepper.

Not to be joked with

While *The Tales* has its humorous side, its content is deadly serious—"not to be joked with."

Noble red pepper

Only here in the story is the red pepper described as noble.

noble: c. 1200, "illustrious, distinguished, of high rank or birth," from Old French *noble* "of noble bearing or birth," from Latin *nobilis* "well-known, famous, renowned; excellent, superior, splendid; high-born, of superior birth," earlier *gnobilis*, literally "knowable," from *gnoscere* "to come to know"

The prominent Roman families, which were "well known," provided most of the Republic's public officials. High-born, but not necessarily high-born in the sense of power-possessing—possibly high-born in the religious sense.

And so, for the purpose of avoiding any misunderstanding through this inherency, the data for which are formed in the entirety of contemporary man, thanks evidently to his frequenting of the cinema and thanks also to his never missing an opportunity of looking into the left eye of the other sex, I wish that this commencing chapter of mine should be printed in the said manner, so that everyone can read it through without cutting the pages of the book itself.

Otherwise the bookseller will, as is said, "cavil," and will without fail again turn out to act in accordance with the basic principle of booksellers in general, formulated by them in the words: "You'll be more of a simpleton than a fisherman if you let go of the fish which has swallowed the bait," and will decline to take back a book whose pages you have cut. I have no doubt of this possibility; indeed, I fully expect such lack of conscience on the part of the booksellers.

And the data for the engendering of my certainty as to this lack of conscience on the part of these booksellers were completely formed in me, when, while I was a professional "Indian Fakir," I needed, for the complete elucidation of a certain "ultra-philosophical" question also to become familiar, among other things, with the associative process for the manifestation of the automatically constructed psyche of contemporary booksellers and of their salesmen when palming off books on their buyers.

Knowing all this and having become, since the misfortune which befell me, habitually just and fastidious in the extreme, I cannot help repeating, or rather, I cannot help again warning you, and even imploringly advising you, before beginning to cut the pages of this first book of mine, to read through very attentively, and even more than once, this first chapter of my writings.

CHAPTER V

The Arousing of Thought 22-28

Contemporary man

And so, for the purpose of avoiding any misunderstanding through this inherency, the data for which are formed in the entirety of contemporary man, thanks evidently to his frequenting of the cinema and thanks also to his never missing an opportunity of looking into the left eye of the other sex, ...

The inherency he is referring to is contemporary man's inherency to thoroughly consume what one has paid for. The cinema was the dominant passive entertainment medium of Gurdjieff's era. The left eye is the "eye of essence." Perhaps this phrase is a reference to sex and flirting being the dominant active means of entertainment.

In *In Search of the Miraculous* Gurdjieff is quoted as saying:

At the same time sex plays a tremendous role in maintaining the mechanicalness of life. Everything that people do is connected with 'sex': politics, religion, art, the theater, music, is all 'sex.'[1]

Cutting the pages

I wish that this commencing chapter of mine should be printed in the said manner, so that everyone can read it through without cutting the pages of the book itself.

Gurdjieff is sure that readers will be inclined to read the book because they paid for it, simply and mechanically, by habit. He does not want such readers. So he wants them to be able to return it, almost as if unread, in the hope of getting their money back.

[1] *In Search of the Miraculous* by P D Ouspensky p254

Booksellers

Otherwise the bookseller will, as is said, "cavil," and will without fail again turn out to act in accordance with the basic principle of booksellers in general, formulated by them in the words:

The text suggests that "booksellers" is metaphorical, suggesting organizations that promote specific ideas and theories, such as for example, Theosophist, Christian Scientists, and other such spiritual movements.

cavil: "to raise frivolous objections, find fault without good reason," 1540s, from Middle French *caviller* "to mock, jest," from Latin *cavillari* "to jeer, mock; satirize, argue scoffingly" (also source of Italian *cavillare*, Spanish *cavilar*), from *cavilla* "jest, jeering," which is related to *calumnia* "slander, false accusation."

Gurdjieff here accuses booksellers of a lack of conscience, although, realistically, if a book's pages have been cut, it is no longer pristine and the bookseller would be justified in refusing to take it back. If taken literally, it does not correspond to a "lack of conscience" by the bookseller. However selling books that advance dubious theories and impractical ideas does.

Fishermen

"You'll be more of a simpleton than a fisherman if you let go of the fish which has swallowed the bait,"

The reference to a fisherman is probably Biblical in the sense of Jesus promising to make his disciples "fishers of men." Those fishers of men were hardly simpletons in the normal sense.

Indian fakir

Gurdjieff wraps these two words in quotes. The point he is making is that the European understanding of what a fakir is and the oriental understanding are different. He expands on this in *Meetings with Remarkable Men* writing:

As I have happened to use the word 'fakir', I do not consider it superfluous to digress a little in order to throw some light on this famous word. It is, indeed, one of the many empty words which, on account of the incorrect meaning given them, particularly in recent times, has an automatic action upon all contemporary Europeans and has become one of the chief causes of the progressive dwindling of their thinking capacity.

Although the word 'fakir' in the meaning given it by Europeans is unknown to the peoples of Asia, nevertheless, this same word is in use there almost everywhere. Fakir, or more correctly fakhr, has as its root the Turkoman word meaning 'beggar', and among almost all the peoples of the continent of Asia whose speech is derived from ancient Turkoman, this word has come down to our day with the meaning of 'swindler' or 'cheat.'

As a matter of fact, to express this meaning of 'swindler' or 'cheat' two different words are used among these peoples, both derived from ancient Turkoman. One is this word 'fakir' and the other is lourie. The former is the word used for a cheat or swindler who uses his guile to take advantage of others by way of their religiousness, while the latter is applied to someone who simply takes advantage of their stupidity. The name lourie, by the way, is given to all gypsies, both as a people and as individuals.[1]

An ultra-philosophical question

Gurdjieff then makes a curious statement about needing to become familiar with booksellers, in order to resolve an ultra-philosophical question. Gurdjieff does not tell the reader what that question was, only that it was ultra-philosophical.

Philosophy: c. 1300, *philosophie*, "knowledge, learning, scholarship, scholarly works, body of knowledge," from Old French *filosofie* "philosophy, knowledge" (12c., Modern French *philosophie*) and directly from Latin *philosophia*, from Greek *philosophia* "love of knowledge, pursuit of wisdom; systematic investigation," from *philo*

[1] *Meetings With Remarkable Men p215*

"loving" + *sophia* "knowledge, wisdom," from *sophis* "wise, learned"; a word of unknown origin. From mid-14c. as "the discipline of dealing in rational speculation or contemplation;" from late 14c. as "natural science," also "alchemy, occult knowledge;" in the Middle Ages the word was understood to embrace all speculative sciences. The meaning "system a person forms for conduct of life" is attested from 1771. The modern sense of "the body of highest truth, the science of the most fundamental matters" is from 1794.

Ultra-: word-forming element of Latin origin meaning "beyond" (ultraviolet, ultrasound), or "extremely, exceedingly" (ultramodern, ultra-religious, from Latin *ultra* (adv. and prep.) "beyond, on the other side, on the farther side, past, over, across."

Even with the above etymological descriptions, it is not clear what Gurdjieff means by ultra-philosophical. Perhaps he is implying that it relates to truth at the highest level.

But in the event that notwithstanding this warning of mine, you should, nevertheless, wish to become acquainted with the further contents of my expositions, then there is already nothing else left for me to do but to wish you with all my "genuine soul" a very, very good appetite, and that you may "digest" all that you read, not only for your own health but for the health of all those near you.

I said "with my genuine soul" because recently living in Europe and coming in frequent contact with people who on every appropriate and inappropriate occasion are fond of taking in vain every sacred name which should belong only to man's inner life, that is to say, with people who swear to no purpose, I being, as I have already confessed, a follower in general not only of the theoretical—as contemporary people have become—but also of the practical sayings of popular wisdom which have become fixed by the centuries, and therefore of the saying which in the present case corresponds to what is expressed by the words: "When you are in Rome do as Rome does," decided, in order not to be out of harmony with the custom established here in Europe of swearing in ordinary conversation, and at the same time to act according to the commandment which was enunciated by the holy lips of Saint Moses "not to take the holy names in vain," to make use of one of those examples of the "newly baked" fashionable languages of the present time, namely English, and so from then on, I began on necessary occasions to swear by my "English soul."

The point is that in this fashionable language, the words "soul" and the bottom of your foot, also called "sole," are pronounced and even written almost alike.

I do not know how it is with you, who are already partly candidate for a buyer of my writings, but my peculiar nature cannot, even with a great mental desire, avoid being indignant at the fact manifested by people

When in Rome

Gurdjieff quotes the usual idiom incorrectly by saying "When you are in Rome do as Rome does." We must presume that he didn't wish to write "when in Rome do as the Romans do." This may be because he has some very critical things to say about the Romans later in *The Tales.*[1]

In the German version, there is an interesting departure in idiom in this passage. The text is: „Mit-den-Wolfen-muß-man-heulen"—literally "with the wolves you must howl."

The commandment

> *... to act according to the commandment which was enunciated by the holy lips of Saint Moses "not to take the holy names in vain,"*

Gurdjieff misquotes the commandment. It's likely that this occasional habit that he adopts is intended to make the reader think about what the commandment actually is.

You can find it twice in the Bible verses Exodus 20:7 and also Deuteronomy 5:11. It is exactly the same in both:

> *Thou shalt not take the name of the LORD thy God in vain; for the LORD will not hold him guiltless that taketh his name in vain.*

> *King James Bible*

Gurdjieff may be extending the commandment to include all holy names or may be referring to the many holy names for the Absolute which he uses throughout *The Tales.*

Soul and sole

> *The point is that in this fashionable language, the words "soul" and the bottom of your foot, also called "sole," are pronounced and even written almost alike.*

sole: "bottom of the human foot" early 14c., from Old French *sole*, from Vulgar Latin *sola*, from Latin *solea* "sandal, bottom of a shoe; a flatfish," from *solum* "bottom,

---

[1] *See second, Chapter XXIX "The Fruits of Former Civilizations and the Blossoms of the Contemporary".*

ground, foundation, lowest point of a thing" (hence "sole of the foot"), a word of uncertain origin.

soul: Middle English *soule*, from Old English *sawol* "spiritual and emotional part of a person, animate existence; life, living being," from Proto-Germanic *saiwalo* (source also of Old Saxon *seola*, Old Norse *sala*, Old Frisian *sele*, Middle Dutch *siele*, Dutch *ziel*, Old High German *seula*, German *Seele*, Gothic *saiwala*), a word of uncertain origin.

The meaning "disembodied spirit of a deceased person" is attested in Old English. As a synonym for "person, individual, human being" (as in every living soul) it dates from early 14c. Soul-searching (n.) "deep self-reflection, examination of one's conscience" is attested from 1871, from the phrase used as a present-participle adjective (1610s).

Gurdjieff regrets the confusion that two words with almost opposite meanings will inevitably create as they have the same consonance.

There is a nuance to Gurdjieff's philologizing about the English words "soul" and "sole"—the meaning of the word "sole" as an adjective. This is the etymology:

sole: "single, alone, having no husband or wife; one and only, singular, unique," late 14c., from Old French *soul* "only, alone, just," from Latin *solus* "alone, only, single, sole; forsaken; extraordinary," of unknown origin, perhaps related to *se* "oneself."

If we review this passage in the German translations of *The Tales*, to see how the English element of it is handled, we see:

English soul is: „englischen-Seele". The words soul, "soul," and sole, "sole of the foot" are: die Worte soul, „Seele," und sole, „Fußsohle."

of contemporary civilization, that the very highest in man, particularly beloved by our COMMON FATHER CRE-ATOR, can really be named, and indeed very often before even having made clear to oneself what it is, can be understood to be that which is lowest and dirtiest in man.

Well, enough of "philologizing." Let us return to the main task of this initial chapter, destined, among other things, on the one hand to stir up the drowsy thoughts in me as well as in the reader, and, on the other, to warn the reader about something.

And so, I have already composed in my head the plan and sequence of the intended expositions, but what form they will take on paper, I, speaking frankly, myself do not as yet know with my consciousness, but with my subconsciousness I already definitely feel that on the whole it will take the form of something which will be, so to say, "hot," and will have an effect on the entirety of every reader such as the red pepper pods had on the poor Transcaucasian Kurd.

Now that you have become familiar with the story of our common countryman, the Transcaucasian Kurd, I already consider it my duty to make a confession and hence before continuing this first chapter, which is by way of an introduction to all my further predetermined writings, I wish to bring to the knowledge of what is called your "pure waking consciousness" the fact that in the writings following this chapter of warning I shall expound my thoughts intentionally in such sequence and with such "logical confrontation," that the essence of certain real notions may of themselves automatically, so to say, go from this "waking consciousness"—which most people in their ignorance mistake for the real consciousness, but which I affirm and experimentally prove is the fictitious one—into what you call the subconscious, which ought to be in my opinion the real human consciousness,

COMMON FATHER CREATOR

... the very highest in man, particularly beloved by our COMMON FATHER CREATOR, ...

This is the first of many references to the Absolute which Gurdjieff makes throughout *The Tales*. The use of full capitalization is a typographical style copied from some versions of the Bible.

Drowsy thoughts

... destined, among other things, on the one hand to stir up the drowsy thoughts in me as well as in the reader, and, on the other, to warn the reader about something.

In *The 1931 Manuscript*, the title of this first chapter was *WARNING (Instead of a Preface)*. This paragraph reflects the idea that both chapter titles were appropriate. It is curious that Gurdjieff claimed that it was destined to have these two effects.

destiny: mid-14c., "fate, over-ruling necessity, the irresistible tendency of certain events to come about; inexorable force that shapes and controls lives and events"; from Old French *destinée* "purpose, intent, fate, destiny; that which is destined" (12c.), noun use of fem. past participle of *destiner*, from Latin *destinare* "make firm, establish". "What is to befall any person or thing in the future" (mid-15c.).

By using the word "destined" he is implying that the first chapter will have an objective impact on the reader. By Gurdjieff's definition, a work of art (such as a book or statue) is objective if it has an identical effect upon everyone that has the same level of being.

In calling the thoughts "drowsy" in respect of both himself and the reader, he is asserting that such thoughts were not the product of active mentation, but will become so.

Hot

... that on the whole it will take the form of something which will be, so to say, "hot," and will have an effect on the entirety of every reader such as the red pepper pods had on the poor Transcaucasian Kurd...

The writing can be considered "hot" in the sense that the effort required to digest and understand it will be great, just as the Kurd's effort was great. The Transcaucasian Kurd is "poor" in the Biblical sense.

Our common countryman

Now that you have become familiar with the story of our common countryman, the Transcaucasian Kurd, ...

"Our common countryman" suggests that we all have a Transcaucasian Kurd within our inner world.

Incidentally, the paragraph that begins in this way is so dense with meaning that we have found it necessary to provide a whole series of notes about it.

My further predetermined writings

... which is by way of an introduction to all my further predetermined writings,

Specifically stating that "The Arousing of Thought" serves as an introduction to all the three series within *ALL and Everything*.

Pure waking consciousness

I wish to bring to the knowledge of what is called your "pure waking consciousness"

Because of the words that follow, by "pure waking consciousness" he must simply mean the second state of consciousness.

Conscious and subconscious

... so to say, go from this "waking consciousness"... ... into what you call the subconscious,

Gurdjieff asserts that what we generally refer to as "our subconscious" ought to be our conscious mind. With the words:

> ... which ought to be in my opinion the real human consciousness,

and

> ...which most people in their ignorance mistake for the real consciousness, but which I affirm and experimentally prove is the fictitious one

Intentional structure of the text of *The Tales*

> ... in the writings following this chapter of warning I shall expound my thoughts intentionally in such sequence and with such "logical confrontation," that the essence of certain real notions may of themselves automatically, go from this "waking consciousness"... ... into what you call the subconscious...

Gurdjieff asserts that the structure of the text, specifically its sequence and the "logical confrontations" that it contains that follow this first chapter will have an objective impact and bring about a transformation in the reader.

and there by themselves mechanically bring about that transformation which should in general proceed in the entirety of a man and give him, from his own conscious mentation, the results he ought to have, which are proper to man and not merely to single- or double-brained animals.

I decided to do this without fail so that this initial chapter of mine, predetermined as I have already said to awaken your consciousness, should fully justify its purpose, and reaching not only your, in my opinion, as yet only fictitious "consciousness," but also your real consciousness, that is to say, what you call your subconscious, might, for the first time, compel you to reflect actively.

In the entirety of every man, irrespective of his heredity and education, there are formed two independent consciousnesses, which in their functioning as well as in their manifestations have almost nothing in common. One consciousness is formed from the perception of all kinds of accidental, or on the part of others intentionally produced, mechanical impressions, among which must also be counted the "consonances" of various words which are indeed as is said empty; and the other consciousness is formed from the so to say, "already previously formed material results" transmitted to him by heredity, which have become blended with the corresponding parts of the entirety of a man, as well as from the data arising from his intentional evoking of the associative confrontations of these "materialized data" already in him.

The whole totality of the formation as well as the manifestation of this second human consciousness, which is none other than what is called the "subconscious," and which is formed from the "materialized results" of heredity and the confrontations actualized by one's own intentions, should in my opinion, formed by many years of my experimental elucidations during exceptionally favorably

That transformation

and there by themselves mechanically bring about that transformation which should in general proceed in the entirety of a man and give him, from his own conscious mentation, the results he ought to have, which are proper to man and not merely to single- or double-brained animals.

The transformation he refers to here is probably the crystallization of the Kesdjan body which is a possibility that man possesses but which one and two-brained beings do not. He promises the reader that his writing will have an impact, not just at the level of personality, but also at the level of essence, and that this "might, for the first time, compel you to reflect actively."

Heredity

In the entirety of every man, irrespective of his heredity and education, ...

heredity: 1530s, "inheritance, succession," from French hérédité, from Old French eredite "inheritance, legacy" (12c.), from Latin hereditatem (nominative hereditas) "heirship, inheritance, an inheritance, condition of being an heir," from heres (genitive heredis) "heir, heiress" (from PIE root ghe- "to be empty, left behind," source also of Greek khera "widow"). Legal sense of "inheritable quality or character" first recorded 1784; the modern biological sense "transmission of qualities from parents to offspring" seems to be found first in 1863, introduced by Herbert Spencer.

It is important for the reader to be aware that Gurdjieff's use of the word "heredity" has no relation to the large body of biological speculation that arose and has developed since the discovery of DNA, which occurred after Gurdjieff's death. When he uses the word he implies what is inherited from family influence.

The first consciousness

> In the entirety of every man, irrespective of his heredity and education, there are formed two independent consciousnesses, which in their functioning as well as in their manifestations have almost nothing in common. One consciousness is formed from the perception of all kinds of accidental, or on the part of others intentionally produced, mechanical impressions, among which must also be counted the "consonances" of various words which are indeed as is said empty;

Here he is describing the consciousness that develops according to mentation by form. This clearly relates to page 15 of *The Tales*, where we read:

> The second kind of mentation, that is, "mentation by form," by which, strictly speaking, the exact sense of all writing must be also perceived, and after conscious confrontation with information already possessed, be assimilated, is formed in people in dependence upon the conditions of geographical locality, climate, time, and, in general, upon the whole environment in which the arising of the given man has proceeded and in which his existence has flowed up to manhood.

Here, however Gurdjieff introduces the idea of consonance. He has referred to consonance once before when noting that the words "sole" and "soul" have the same consonance. Here he asserts that in the formation of this first kind of consciousness the consonance of words that contribute to its formation are valueless, because the meaning of the word has not yet been digested.

The second consciousness

> and the other consciousness is formed from the so to say, "already previously formed material results" transmitted to him by heredity, which have become blended with the corresponding parts of the entirety of a man, as well as from the data arising from his intentional evoking of the

associative confrontations of these "materialized data" already in him.

Here he is describing the consciousness that develops at least partly according to mentation by thought. We refer again to page 15 of *The Tales*, where we read:

one kind, mentation by thought, in which words, always possessing a relative sense, are employed

The second consciousness is formed by heredity—in other words experiences that were gathered from family and culture during childhood. We read this paragraph to mean "only those data which *have become blended with the corresponding parts of the entirety of a man* (that is, his three brains) and data arising from his experiences which he has intentionally digested."

In Gurdjieff's view, this second consciousness forms the subconsciousness of contemporary man.

arranged conditions, predominate in the common presence of a man.

As a result of this conviction of mine which as yet doubtlessly seems to you the fruit of the fantasies of an afflicted mind, I cannot now, as you yourself see, disregard this second consciousness and, compelled by my essence, am obliged to construct the general exposition even of this first chapter of my writings, namely, the chapter which should be the preface for everything further, calculating that it should reach and, in the manner required for my aim, "ruffle" the perceptions accumulated in both these consciousnesses of yours.

Continuing my expositions with this calculation, I must first of all inform your fictitious consciousness that, thanks to three definite peculiar data which were crystallized in my entirety during various periods of my preparatory age, I am really unique in respect of the so to say "muddling and befuddling" of all the notions and convictions supposedly firmly fixed in the entirety of people with whom I come in contact.

Tut! Tut! Tut! ... I already feel that in your "false"— but according to you "real"—consciousness, there are beginning to be agitated, like "blinded flies," all the chief data transmitted to you by heredity from your uncle and mother, the totality of which data, always and in everything, at least engenders in you the impulse—nevertheless extremely good—of curiosity, as in the given case, to find out as quickly as possible why I, that is to say, a novice at writing, whose name has not even once been mentioned in the newspapers, have suddenly become so unique.

Never mind! I personally am very pleased with the arising of this curiosity even though only in your "false" consciousness, as I already know from experience that this impulse unworthy of man can sometimes even pass from this consciousness into one's nature and become a

Ruffle

in the manner required for my aim, "ruffle" the perceptions accumulated in both these consciousnesses of yours.

ruffle: early 14c., *ruffelen*, "to disturb the smoothness or order of," a word of obscure origin. Similar forms are found in Scandinavian (such as Old Norse *hrufla* "to scratch") and Low German (*ruffelen* "to wrinkle, curl;" Middle Low German *ruffen* "to fornicate"), but the exact relation and origin of them is uncertain. Also compare Middle English *ruffelen* "be at odds with, quarrel, dispute." The meaning "disarrange" (hair or feathers) is recorded from late 15c.; the sense of "annoy, vex, distract" is from 1650s.

He states that his writing will impact both consciousnesses and directly shock (ruffle) them.

Three definite peculiar data

...thanks to three definite peculiar data which were crystallized in my entirety during various periods of my preparatory age, I am really unique in respect of the so to say "muddling and befuddling" of all the notions and convictions supposedly firmly fixed in the entirety of people with whom I come in contact.

He introduces here the idea that he will be adept at ruffling these two different consciousnesses because of the influence on him of three significant events that occurred to him in his childhood and youth.

muddle: 1590s, "destroy the clarity of" (a transferred sense); literal sense ("to bathe in mud") is from c. 1600; perhaps frequentative formation from mud, or from Dutch *moddelen* "to make (water) muddy," from the same Proto-Germanic source. Sense of "to make muddy" is from 1670s; that of "make confused, bewilder" is recorded by 1680s. Meaning "to bungle" is from 1885. Related: muddled; muddling.

befuddle: 1832 "to confuse with strong drink or opium." 1873, "confuse," from *be-* + *fuddle*. *Fuddle*, 1580s, "to get drunk" (intransitive); c. 1600, "to confuse as though with drink" (transitive), perhaps from Low German *fuddeln* "work in a slovenly manner (as if drunk)," from *fuddle* "worthless cloth." A hard-drinker in 17c. might be called a fuddle-cap (1660s).

"Muddling and befuddling" is a poetic way of describing his ability to impact the reader.

Like "blinded flies"

I already feel that in your "false"...consciousness, there are beginning to be agitated, like "blinded flies," all the chief data transmitted to you by heredity from your uncle and mother, the totality of which data, always and in everything, at least engenders in you the impulse ...of curiosity... to find out as quickly as possible why I ...have suddenly become so unique.

The expression "like blinded flies" is generally used to describe people or things moving around haphazardly, aimlessly, or in a confused, chaotic manner. Blinded flies would buzz and bump into things without direction or purpose.

In this case he is most likely referring to thoughts, ideas, or impulses that are stirred up without conscious direction, like blinded flies.

Mentioned in newspapers

whose name has not even once been mentioned in the newspapers,

This is historically incorrect. Gurdjieff was mentioned on quite a few occasions in U.S. newspapers from 1921 onwards, particularly following his first visit in 1924. This is yet another example of theatrical inexactitude.

This curiosity

I personally am very pleased with the arising of this curiosity even though only in your "false" consciousness, as I already know from experience that this impulse unworthy of man can sometimes even pass from this consciousness into one's nature and become a worthy impulse—the impulse of the desire for knowledge, ...

The text implies that Gurdjieff is convinced that he has aroused this curiosity in the reader's "false" consciousness because he knows that such curiosity can establish in the reader's nature a desire for knowledge.

The desire for knowledge

the desire for knowledge, which, in its turn, assists the better perception and even the closer understanding of the essence of any object on which, as it sometimes happens, the attention of a contemporary man might be concentrated, and therefore I am even willing, with pleasure, to satisfy this curiosity which has arisen in you at the present moment.

Gurdjieff asserts that the desire for knowledge can improve the digestion of impressions and concentrate the attention.

worthy impulse—the impulse of the desire for knowledge, which, in its turn, assists the better perception and even the closer understanding of the essence of any object on which, as it sometimes happens, the attention of a contemporary man might be concentrated, and therefore I am even willing, with pleasure, to satisfy this curiosity which has arisen in you at the present moment.

Now listen and try to justify, and not to disappoint, my expectations. This original personality of mine, already "smelled out" by certain definite individuals from both choirs of the Judgment Seat Above, whence Objective justice proceeds, and also here on Earth, by as yet a very limited number of people, is based, as I already said, on three secondary specific data formed in me at different times during my preparatory age. The first of these data, from the very beginning of its arising, became as it were the chief directing lever of my entire wholeness, and the other two, the "vivifying-sources," as it were, for the feeding and perfecting of this first datum.

The arising of this first datum proceeded when I was still only, as is said, a "chubby mite." My dear now deceased grandmother was then still living and was a hundred and some years old.

When my grandmother—may she attain the kingdom of Heaven—was dying, my mother, as was then the custom, took me to her bedside, and as I kissed her right hand, my dear now deceased grandmother placed her dying left hand on my head and in a whisper, yet very distinctly, said:

"Eldest of my grandsons! Listen and always remember my strict injunction to you: In life never do as others do." Having said this, she gazed at the bridge of my nose and evidently noticing my perplexity and my obscure understanding of what she had said, added somewhat angrily and imposingly:

This original personality of mine

This original personality of mine, already "smelled out" by certain definite individuals from both choirs of the Judgment Seat Above, whence Objective justice proceeds, and also here on Earth, by as yet a very limited number of people, is based, as I already said, on three secondary specific data formed in me at different times during my preparatory age.

The term to "smell out" generally means to find something out through intuition, subtle clues, or experience, rather than direct evidence. It carries a sense of "nosing out" or "scenting out" a situation.

Gurdjieff attaches initial capitals to the "Judgement Seat Above," indicating importance. In a biblical context the term may refer to the divine court or tribunal where Christ (or God) acts as the ultimate judge of all humanity. New testament references for this are:

2 Corinthians 5:10. For we must all appear before the judgment seat of Christ; that every one may receive the things done in his body, according to that he hath done, whether it be good or bad.

Romans 14:10. But why dost thou judge thy brother? or why dost thou set at nought thy brother? for we shall all stand before the judgment seat of Christ.

We were unable to unearth any references to "both choirs" in relation to the "Judgement Seat Above," or in relation to any Christian texts. He may be inventing the idea.

Chubby mite

To satisfy this description Gurdjieff would have had to be very young, perhaps four years old, and preschool age.

One hundred and some years old.

My dear now deceased grandmother was then still living and was a hundred and some years old.

The age given is highly likely to be a theatrical exaggeration—the age difference could not have been so great. Nevertheless it is worth noting here that Gurdjieff had a remarkable grandmother, to whom Tcheslaw Tchekhovitch devoted several pages in his book: *Gurdjieff, A Master in Life*.[1]

According to Tchekhovitch's account she was a talented, well-respected and renowned midwife, and may indeed have given Gurdjieff advice that stayed with him. Tchekhovitch describes her death in the following way:

> When she felt her end approaching due to cancer of the liver, she devoted herself entirely to prayer, wishing to remain conscious and lucid in the face of death. After several days, sensing that her final hour was imminent, she prepared her body for death, dressed herself in a gown that would serve as her shroud, and quietly lay down to await the end. Even as her body was getting cold, she chanted the words of her favourite prayer, "Our Father who art in Heaven, hallowed be Thy name...," sometimes looking at those present as if to assure herself that she was still here on earth, sometimes singing more loudly, "Thy Kingdom come ...," as if to let the mystery resound more deeply in herself.

> Her last words, spoken in Armenian, had the character of a Japanese poem;
> The bird is silent.
> It has flown away
> To the other land
> The flower has faded.
> It has left this life,

> But the wind will scatter its seeds.

> And looking at those around her, she added, "And you! Laugh or cry. Do as you wish. It's all the same to me. I am already elsewhere."

> After uttering these words, she closed her eyes, never to open them again.

---

[1] *Gurdjieff, A Master in Life*, pp237 - 240

It is also important to note that elsewhere Gurdjieff uses "grandmother"' as a symbol of wisdom, passed down within the family.

Never do as others do

"Eldest of my grandsons! Listen and always remember my strict injunction to you: In life never do as others do."

Having said this, she gazed at the bridge of my nose and evidently noticing my perplexity and my obscure understanding of what she had said, added somewhat angrily and imposingly:

"Either do nothing—just go to school—or do something nobody else does."

Such an event would naturally be unforgettable, in the life of a child.

"Either do nothing—just go to school—or do something nobody else does."

Whereupon she immediately, without hesitation, and with a perceptible impulse of disdain for all around her, and with commendable self-cognizance, gave up her soul directly into the hands of His Truthfulness, the Archangel Gabriel.

Archangel Gabriel

...with commendable self-cognizance, gave up her soul directly into the hands of His Truthfulness, the Archangel Gabriel.

The Archangel Gabriel no doubt deserves the title His Truthfulness that Gurdjieff confers on him. However he is not normally associated with receiving the souls of the dead.

In religious tradition, Gabriel's central role is to deliver God's most critical messages and revelations to humanity, often concerning future events or divine plans.

In The New Testament: He is best known for his appearance to the Virgin Mary to announce that she would conceive and bear Jesus. He also appears to the priest Zechariah to announce the miraculous birth of his son, John the Baptist (Luke 1:11-20). As he has the role of herald, he was designated the patron saint of messengers, communication workers, postal workers, and telecommunications in general.

In Judaism (Hebrew Bible/Old Testament), Gabriel appears to the Prophet Daniel to explain and interpret complex visions and prophecies concerning the future of Israel. He is often viewed as an angel of strength and is sometimes associated with divine justice, such as in the destruction of Sodom and Gomorrah.

The name Gabriel (from the Hebrew Gabriʾēl) is generally interpreted as "God is my strength" or "Strong Man of God."

In Islam (Quran): He is known as Jibrīl (or Jabrāʾīl), and he holds the highest rank among the angels.

He is the primary agent of divine revelation, responsible for dictating the verses of the holy book, the Qur'an, to the Prophet Muhammad over a period of 23 years.

—— 006 ——

I think it will be interesting and even instructive to you to know that all this made so powerful an impression on me at that time that I suddenly became unable to endure anyone around me, and therefore, as soon as we left the room where the mortal "planetary body" of the cause of the cause of my arising lay, I very quietly, trying not to attract attention, stole away to the pit where during Lent the bran and potato skins for our "sanitarians," that is to say, our pigs, were stored, and lay there, without food or drink, in a tempest of whirling and confused thoughts— of which, fortunately for me, I had then in my childish brain still only a very limited number—right until the return from the cemetery of my mother, whose weeping on finding me gone and after searching for me in vain, as it were "overwhelmed" me. I then immediately emerged from the pit and standing first of all on the edge, for some reason or other with outstretched hand, ran to her and clinging fast to her skirts, involuntarily began to stamp my feet and why, I don't know, to imitate the braying of the donkey belonging to our neighbor, a bailiff.

Why this produced such a strong impression on me just then, and why I almost automatically manifested so strangely, I cannot until now make out; though during recent years, particularly on the days called "Shrovetide," I pondered a good deal, trying chiefly to discover the reason for it.

I then had only the logical supposition that it was perhaps only because the room in which this sacred scene

CHAPTER VI

The Arousing of Thought 28-35

Planetary body

In Gurdjieffian terminology, the "planetary body" is the lowest of the three "being-bodies" possessed by a Man, or a three-brained being. It refers to the physical body itself—the purely material and instinctive vehicle that is mortal, as the text declares. The two higher bodies are the "Kesdjan body" (or astral body) which is generally incomplete and the "Soul body" which is also incomplete. These two higher bodies can be perfected or crystallized and thus become permanent.

Sanitarians

Traditionally Armenians in rural villages tended to keep pigs on a family or small household basis. In referring to pigs as "sanitarians," Gurdjieff is drawing attention to their usefulness. They were and still are to some degree in rural areas an efficient source of meat and fat (lard) for the family They reproduce quickly and can be maintained on a diet of agricultural by-products and food scraps.

During Lent, the pigs' diet would be limited to vegetable waste (potato peel and bran is likely) and this would be stored in a different bin than normal pig food. In Armenia, pigs were typically raised throughout the year and then slaughtered in the late autumn or early winter, providing the family with a large stock of meat and preserved products (like cured ham and sausages) for the coming months.

The Armenian Lent

The Armenian Orthodox Great Lent is known as *Medz Bahk*, which translates to "great fast." It is sometimes referred to as *Aghoohats,* which translates to "salt and bread"—the strictest observers of Lent hold to that meagre diet, plus water.

However the guidelines for what observers of Great Lent are generally allowed to eat is: vegetables and fruits (fresh or dried), grains and legumes (bread, rice, wheat, bulgur, beans, lentils, chickpeas, etc.), other plant-based foods, vegetable oils and honey. Beverages include fruit juice, coffee, tea, and water. Forbiden foods include all flesh meats and animal products, including eggs, milk and other dairy products, all fish and all alcoholic beverages.

Armenian Shrovetide

The Armenian equivalent of Shrovetide is *Poon Barekendan.* It falls on the final Sunday before the beginning of Great Lent.

The literal meaning of *Poon* is "main" or "genuine" while *Barekendan* means "kind life" or "good life," symbolizing the joy and plenitude of life in the Garden of Eden before the fall of Adam and Eve.

Similar to Mardi Gras, *Poon Barekendan* is a day of festivity, merriment, and feasting, particularly on everything that is strictly prohibited during Great Lent.

On the Saturday evening preceding Barekendan Sunday, the altar curtain in Armenian churches is ceremonially closed and remains closed until Palm Sunday, symbolizing the expulsion of Adam and Eve from Paradise (the main altar symbolizes the Throne of God).

The burial

... right until the return from the cemetery of my mother, whose weeping on finding me gone and after searching for me in vain, as it were "overwhelmed" me.

The Armenian tradition is to bury the dead three days after death. The deceased's body is often kept at home until the burial, where a wake, or *Dan Gark*, is held the night before the funeral. This time allows for the preparation of the body, the wake, and for relatives and friends to gather.

The text implies that Gurdjieff hid himself away for three days—confused by the events he had experienced. His mother missed him when the funeral was over.

Not doing as others do

I then immediately emerged from the pit and standing first of all on the edge, for some reason or other with outstretched hand, ran to her and clinging fast to her skirts, involuntarily began to stamp my feet and why, I don't know, to imitate the braying of the donkey belonging to our neighbor, a bailiff.

This can be taken as the first example of Gurdjieff not doing as others do. However it can be interpreted differently. A young child clings to their mother's long skirt for safety, to avoid a frightening situation. A donkey is a symbol of the lower self which is usually obstinate and stuck in its ways. A "bailiff" is an officer of the law whose job it is to see that debts are paid—the neighboring bailiff may signify one who is concerned with higher justice.

Shrovetide

Since Gurdjieff uses the word "shrovetide," it's worth noting its etymology.

shrove: "shrift, shriving," 1570s, used only in ecclesiastical phrases, shortened from Shrovetide (early 15c., *Shrof-tide*), "the three days before Ash Wednesday," a time of confession, from *schrof-*, which is related to *schrifen* and *shrive* (which means to confess). Shrove Tuesday (c. 1500, earlier *Shrof-dai*, mid-15c.) is from practice of celebration and merrymaking before confession at the start of Lent.

occurred, which was to have tremendous significance for the whole of my further life, was permeated through and through with the scent of a special incense brought from the monastery of "Old Athos" and very popular among followers of every shade of belief of the Christian religion. Whatever it may have been, this fact still now remains a bare fact.

During the days following this event, nothing particular happened in my general state, unless there might be connected with it the fact that during these days, I walked more often than usual with my feet in the air, that is to say, on my hands.

My first act, obviously in discordance with the manifestations of others, though truly without the participation not only of my consciousness but also of my subconsciousness, occurred on exactly the fortieth day after the death of my grandmother, when all our family, our relatives and all those by whom my dear grandmother, who was loved by everybody, had been held in esteem, gathered in the cemetery according to custom, to perform over her mortal remains, reposing in the grave, what is called the "requiem service," when suddenly without any rhyme or reason, instead of observing what was conventional among people of all degrees of tangible and intangible morality and of all material positions, that is to say, instead of standing quietly as if overwhelmed, with an expression of grief on one's face and even if possible with tears in one's eyes, I started skipping round the grave as if dancing, and sang:

"Let her with the saints repose,
Now that she's turned up her toes,
Oi! oi! oi!
Let her with the saints repose,
Now that she's turned up her toes."

Fig 5. The location of Mount Athos (courtesy Google Maps)

Mount Athos

because the room in which this sacred scene occurred, which was to have tremendous significance for the whole of my further life, was permeated through and through with the scent of a special incense brought from the monastery of "Old Athos" and very popular among followers of every shade of belief of the Christian religion.

Mount Athos, or the Holy Mountain (Ayion Óros), is a self-governed monastic state in Greece and the spiritual heart of Eastern Orthodox monasticism.

It has its origin in the 4th century when hermits and ascetics began settling on the remote peninsula. By the late 9th century, small monastic communities (lavras) had emerged. In 885 AD, an edict by Byzantine Emperor Basil I officially proclaimed Athos a place exclusively for monks.

The famous rule forbidding all women (and female animals) from the peninsula, known as the Avaton, was decided during this early period. According to tradition, the Virgin Mary claimed the mountain as her own garden (Theotokos's Garden).

179

The official beginning of organized monasticism is marked by the founding of the Great Lavra monastery in 963 AD by Saint Athanasios the Athonite. This became the first and largest of the ruling monasteries. Subsequently numerous other major monasteries were established. The Byzantine Emperors granted the monasteries extensive wealth, privileges, and protection.

Monks from various Orthodox nations, including Georgia, Russia, and Serbia, flocked to Athos, establishing their own monasteries. The 14th century saw the rise and triumph of the Hesychast movement—a mystical tradition focused on inner stillness and the Jesus Prayer—championed by Saint Gregory Palamas.

Despite the fall of Constantinople to the Ottoman Turks in 1453, the monasteries were generally allowed to continue their existence, often in exchange for heavy taxes. So, Athos became a crucial cultural and intellectual refuge, safeguarding Orthodox Christian identity and preserving invaluable manuscripts and art.

Today, Mount Athos remains an autonomous monastic republic, recognized as a UNESCO World Heritage Site since 1988, continuing its thousand-year-old tradition of prayer, asceticism, and preservation of Orthodox faith and culture.

The scent of a special incense

In Armenia, incense would not normally be burnt in the room of a dying person, but would be a core element of the wake (or Dan Gark). Burning incense around the open casket symbolizes prayers rising to heaven and signifies the enduring presence of God among the mourners.

The tradition of producing incense on Mount Athos is ancient, stretching back to the 10th century. The incense is handmade following centuries-old traditional recipes and techniques known as the "Athonite style." It is considered a part of the monks' prayer and offering in worship.

The base ingredient is usually frankincense resin (also called olibanum), which is the dried sap of the Boswellia tree, often imported from Western Africa or the Arabian Peninsula. This resin is combined with a powder (such as magnesium) and essential aromatic oils or fragrances. The mixture is worked into a paste, dried, and then cut into small pieces.

Mount Athos incense is highly regarded for its superior quality, clean burn, and rich, long-lasting aromas. Authentic pieces are generally hard to the touch and less powdery than some imitations.

Requiem service

gathered in the cemetery according to custom, to perform over her mortal remains, reposing in the grave, what is called the "requiem service,"

requiem: "mass for repose of the soul of the dead," c. 1300, from Latin *requiem*, accusative singular of *requiescere* "rest (after labor), be idle, repose," from *re-* + *quiescere* "to repose, rest, sleep," from *quies* "quiet." It is the first word of the Mass for the Dead in the Latin liturgy: *Requiem æternam dona eis, Domine* .... ["Rest eternal grant them, O Lord ..."]

The requiem service carried out for the dead in Armenia (within the Armenian Apostolic Church) is a very important and deeply respected tradition. It is called Hokehankist (or Hokehankeesd), which means "repose of the soul."

It is usually held on the 40th day (Karasoonk) and marks the end of the official mourning period.

An enigmatic assertion

... though truly without the participation not only of my consciousness but also of my subconsciousness, ...

Given this assertion, it is difficult to pinpoint or even guess whence came the motivation to skip around the grave and sing.

Conventional behavior

... instead of observing what was conventional among people of all degrees of tangible and intangible morality and

of all material positions, that is to say, instead of standing quietly as if overwhelmed, with an expression of grief on one's face and even if possible with tears in one's eyes,

Gurdjieff homes in on the fact that in such circumstances at least some of those present will be insincere in their behavior. If one believes that the deceased has ascended rather than descended, then to be happy for them is logical. Genuine expressions of grief will most likely be in respect of one's own loss. Insincere expressions of grief are most likely inner considering.

Skipping and dancing

I started skipping round the grave as if dancing, and sang:

"Let her with the saints repose,
Now that she's turned up her toes,
Oi! oi! oi!
Let her with the saints repose,
Now that she's turned up her toes."

This "poem" is probably the work of Orage. However, while it is unexpected behavior—as the text insists—it is not disrespectful.

... obviously in discordance with the manifestations of others, ...

He wishes that her soul rest with the saints now that she is dead.

As you might suspect, the poem doesn't translate to other languages. For example, the German text is:

„Mit allen Heiligen Im Himmelreich
Hier kam ihr kein anderer gleich... Ei, ei, ei!
Mit allen Heiligen im Himmelreich
Hier kam ihr kein anderer gleich... «

Which translates to:

"With all the saints in the kingdom of heaven,
no one else could compare to her... Oh, oh, oh!

*With all the saints in the kingdom of heaven,
no one else could compare to her..."*

... and so on and so forth.

And just from this it began, that in my entirety a "something" arose which in respect of any kind of so to say "aping," that is to say, imitating the ordinary automatized manifestations of those around me, always and in everything engendered what I should now call an "irresistible urge" to do things not as others do them.

At that age I committed acts such as the following.

If for example when learning to catch a ball with the right hand, my brother, sisters and the neighbors' children who came to play with us, threw the ball in the air, I, with the same aim in view, would first bounce the ball hard on the ground, and only when it rebounded would I, first doing a somersault, catch it, and then only with the thumb and middle finger of the left hand; or if all the other children slid down the hill head first, I tried to do it, and moreover each time better and better, as the children then called it, "backside-first"; or if we children were given various kinds of what are called "Abaranian pastries," then all the other children, before putting them in their mouths, would first of all lick them, evidently to try their taste and to protract the pleasure, but ... I would first sniff one on all sides and perhaps even put it to my ear and listen intently, and then though only almost unconsciously, yet nevertheless seriously, muttering to myself "so and so and so you must, do not eat until you bust," and rhythmically humming correspondingly, I would only take one bite and without savoring it, would swallow it—and so on and so forth.

The first event during which there arose in me one of the two mentioned data which became the "vivifying sources" for the feeding and perfecting of the injunction of my deceased grandmother, occurred just at that age when I changed from a chubby mite into what is called a "young rascal" and had already begun to be, as is sometimes

Fig 6. Map of Armenia showing Gyumri (formerly Alexandropol) and
Aparan. (courtesy Google Maps)

Abaranian pastries

*... or if we children were given various kinds of what are
called "Abaranian pastries,"...*

The area historically known as Abaran in Armenia is today
the town of Aparan. The town's name was changed from
Abaran in 1935. The name Aparan is commonly believed to
be derived from the Armenian word *aparank*, meaning "royal
palace."

Aparan is well known for being home to the Gntuniq
Bakery. It is a popular and historic stop along the major M3
highway that runs through Aparan. Travelers stop there for its
fresh baked goods. The Gntuniq Bakery is especially famous
for its Gata (Armenian sweet bread) and the Lavash
(traditional Armenian flatbread), which are often baked in a
traditional clay oven called a Tonir. The sheer variety and
quality of its bread and pastries have made the town a minor
culinary landmark in the region.

Imitating the product of the Gntuniq Bakery, Abaranian
pastries, (Gata) are made elsewhere in Armenia. The dough is
made with flour, butter, sugar, eggs, and sometimes matsuni
(Armenian yogurt) or sour cream, which gives it a tender

texture. The filling is a mixture of flour, butter, sugar, walnuts, vanilla and spices like cinnamon.

Young rascal

what is called a "young rascal" and had already begun to be, as is sometimes said, a "candidate for a young man of pleasing appearance and dubious content."

rascal: The word entered Middle English as *rascaile*, meaning "people of the lowest class" or the "rabble of an army." It derived from the Old French word *rascaille*, which meant "outcast" or "rabble" (modern French *racaille*). The Old French word is thought to potentially come from Vulgar Latin *rasicō* ("to scrape"), or perhaps Old French *rasque* ("mud, filth, scab, dregs"). In the present-day, it is often used in the affectionate sense of a "cheeky, mischievous person or creature," from the early 17th century onwards.

Gurdjieff is using the word "rascal" in the more modern sense of mischievous, both in respect of himself and his friends, noting that an adolescent boy is often a candidate for "a young man of pleasing appearance and dubious content."

said, a "candidate for a young man of pleasing appearance and dubious content."

And this event occurred under the following circumstances, which were perhaps even specially combined by Fate itself.

With a number of young rascals like myself, I was once laying snares for pigeons on the roof of a neighbor's house, when suddenly, one of the boys who was standing over me and watching me closely, said:

"I think the noose of the horsehair ought to be so arranged that the pigeon's big toe never gets caught in it, because, as our zoology teacher recently explained to us, during movement it is just in that toe that the pigeon's reserve strength is concentrated, and therefore if this big toe gets caught in the noose, the pigeon might of course easily break it."

Another boy, leaning just opposite me, from whose mouth, by the way, whenever he spoke saliva always splashed abundantly in all directions, snapped at this remark of the first boy and delivered himself, with a copious quantity of saliva, of the following words:

"Shut your trap, you hopeless mongrel offshoot of the Hottentots! What an abortion you are, just like your teacher! Suppose it is true that the greatest physical force of the pigeon is concentrated in that big toe, then all the more, what we've got to do is to see that just that toe will be caught in the noose. Only then will there be any sense to our aim—that is to say, for catching these unfortunate pigeon creatures—in that brain-particularity proper to all possessors of that soft and slippery 'something' which consists in this, that when, thanks to other actions, from which its insignificant manifestability depends, there arises a periodic requisite law-conformable what is called 'change of presence,' then this small so to say 'law-conformable confusion' which should proceed for the animation of

Fate

And this event occurred under the following circum-stances, which were perhaps even specially combined by Fate itself.

In reviewing the life of a man (including one's own life), it is often difficult to know which (if any) events are the "will of Fate." Note that Gurdjieff capitalizes the word "fate," indicating something of a higher nature. It is easy to fantasize about events being "directed by fate" when in truth they are simply a matter of accident—there is no easy way to distinguish one possibility from the other.

From the perspective of the Work, if we accept that the whole of reality unquestionably obeys the Law of Three, then it is difficult to view oneself (or anyone else) as controlling one's destiny. The theory that fate is a participating force is credible.

Pigeons

In practice, there is little to distinguish between a pigeon and a dove. Gurdjieff is possibly playing with the reader here, as the dove is a potent symbol in Christianity.

Its most prominent appearance is at Jesus' Baptism. All four Gospels record the Holy Spirit descending upon Jesus in the form of a dove as he is baptised by John the Baptist. The dove is thus a symbolic representation of the third person of the Trinity.

And the Holy Spirit descended on him in bodily form like a dove."

(Luke 3:22)

Also Jesus advised his disciples to have this dual nature:

Be wise as serpents and innocent as doves."

(Matthew 10:16)

We also encounter the dove in The Old Testament. After the Great Flood, Noah sent out a dove. The dove returned with an olive branch in its beak, signaling that the waters had receded and that God's judgment was over. The dove with an olive branch subsequently became a universal symbol of peace, hope, and new beginnings.

In early Christian art, especially in the catacombs and on sarcophagi, the dove often represented the peace of the soul: it signified the peaceful state of a deceased person's soul in Christ.

If you're thinking "what has this to do with pigeons", the answer is "quite a lot." Scientifically, there is no distinction between a dove and pigeon. They both belong to the same biological family, Columbidae, which contains over 300 species.

The different words are normally used based on size, and possibly cultural context.

Typically, the word "dove" is used to designate the smaller, more delicate species with a slender neck and a tapered tail, like the common mourning dove. Whereas "pigeon" is used to refer to the larger, stockier species with a bulkier body and a shorter, squarer tail which tend to congregate in cities and are rock doves.

The etymologies of the words does not help. "Dove" comes from Germanic languages (Old Norse: *dufa*). "Pigeon" comes from French (Latin: *pipio*). Both words survived in English, leading to the confusion that exists.

On the roof

With a number of young rascals like myself, I was once laying snares for pigeons on the roof of a neighbor's house, when suddenly, one of the boys who was standing over me and watching me closely, ...

roof: "outer upper covering of a house or other building," Middle English *rof*, from Old English *hrof* "roof," also "ceiling," hence figuratively "highest point, top, summit" also "heaven, the sky;" from Proto-Germanic *khrofam* (source also of Old Frisian *rhoof* "roof," Middle Dutch *roof*, *rouf* "cover, roof," Dutch *roef* "deckhouse, cabin, coffin-lid," Middle High German *rof* "penthouse," Old Norse *hrof* "boat shed").

It is surprising that the etymology includes "the sky and heaven." In Armenia many houses have flat roofs with earth on top, so it is quite possible that a group of boys would try to catch pigeons on a roof, although it would make more sense to try to snare them on the ground.

> **snare:** "noose for catching animals," late Old English *snearu*, and also from a Scandinavian source such as Old Norse *snara* "noose, snare," related to *soenri* "twisted rope," from Proto-Germanic *snarkho* (source also of Middle Dutch *snare*, Dutch *snaar*, Old High German *snare*, German *Schnur* "noose, cord," Old English *snear* "a string, cord"). Figuratively from c. 1300, "anything by which one is entangled or entrapped."

Of a neighbor's house

In Christianity, the "neighbor" is a central concept, rooted in the command to "Love your neighbor as yourself." Jesus identified this commandment (from Leviticus 19:18) as the second greatest commandment:

> Then one of them, which was a lawyer, asked him a question, tempting him, and saying,
>
> Master, which is the great commandment in the law?
>
> Jesus said unto him, Thou shalt love the Lord thy God with all thy heart, and with all thy soul, and with all thy mind.
>
> This is the first and great commandment.
>
> And the second is like unto it, Thou shalt love thy neighbour as thyself.
>
> On these two commandments hang all the law and the prophets.
>
> Matthew 22:35 - 22:39

In Jesus's Parable of the Good Samaritan (Luke 10:25-37), the idea that one's neighbor is someone who lives physically close by is laid to rest.

The horsehair noose

"I think the noose of the horsehair ought to be so arranged that the pigeon's big toe never gets caught in it,

The horsehair snare is a traditional method for catching small songbirds. The hair from a horse's tail, is surprisingly strong for a natural fiber. Because of this it has been used for things like fishing line, bowstrings for musical instruments, and as a reinforcement fiber.

However, the traditional horsehair snare is not as Gurdjieff describes. It involves a fine loop made from braided horse tail hair placed near attractive bait, like seeds or berries. The loop is so arranged that when the bird lowers its head to take the bait, the loop falls over its neck. When the bird attempts to fly away, the hair loop tightens, leading to strangulation.

A pigeon is too large a bird for such a trap. For such prey it is more effective to set up a box or cage-based trap. The discussion about trapping the pigeon by its toes probably doesn't relate to a real event.

Horsehair is mentioned later in *The Tales*, on p851, in the description of the Lav-Merz-Nokh. The horse symbolizes emotion.

Pigeons/doves, along with most other birds, have a toe arrangement suited to perching on twigs of trees, with three toes pointing forward and one long toe pointing back—the hallux, which is the equivalent of the big toe in humans.

Saliva

Another boy, leaning just opposite me, from whose mouth, by the way, whenever he spoke saliva always splashed abundantly in all directions, snapped at this remark of the first boy and delivered himself, with a copious quantity of saliva, ...

We may wish to think of this group of boys as Gurdjieff's "many I's" debating various topics. The splashing of saliva while speaking tends to go along with speaking loudly and with great emphasis—this increases the velocity and turbulence of expelled air, which could naturally lead to saliva droplets being launched.

Hottentots

"Shut your trap, you hopeless mongrel offshoot of the Hottentots! What an abortion you are, just like your teacher!

Mongrel: mid-15c., "individual or breed of dog resulting from repeated crossings or mixture of several different varieties," from obsolete *mong* "mixture," from Old English *gemong* "mingling" (base of among), from Proto-Germanic *mangjan* "to knead together" (source of mingle). The distinction between a mongrel and a hybrid (a cross between two different breeds) is not always observed. The meaning "person not of pure race" is attested from 1540s. As an adjective, "of a mixed or impure breed," from 1570s.

Hottentot: 1670s, from South African Dutch, said in old Dutch sources to be a word that means "stammerer," from *hot en tot* "hot and tot," nonsense words imitative of stammering. The word was applied to the people for the clicking, jerking quality of Khoisan speech.

This outright insult "hopeless mongrel offshoot of the Hottentots" is common in unsophisticated arguments where the arguer prefers to insult his opponent rather than debate in a logical manner. However, this insult is followed by a very difficult to understand and maybe even sophisticated assertion... as follows:

Soft and slippery something

Suppose it is true that the greatest physical force of the pigeon is concentrated in that big toe, then all the more, what we've got to do is to see that just that toe will be caught in the noose. Only then will there be any sense to our aim—that is to say, for catching these unfortunate pigeon creatures—in that brain-particularity proper to all possessors of that soft and slippery 'something' which consists in this, that when, thanks to other actions, from which its insignificant manifestability depends, there arises a periodic requisite law-conformable what is called 'change of presence,' then this small so to say 'law-conformable confusion' which should proceed for the animation of other acts in its general functioning, immediately enables the center of gravity of the whole functioning, in which this slippery 'something' plays a very small part, to pass temporarily from its usual place to another place, owing to which there often obtains in the whole of this general functioning, unexpected results ridiculous to the point of absurdity."

A question that naturally arises is whether this collection of bewildering words actually has a meaning that the reader can delve into, or whether Gurdjieff is simply trying to baffle or even intimidate the reader.

Breaking this paragraph down:

- The boy proposes that it is better to snare the big toe of the pigeon, and that only then will there be any sense to their aim of catching pigeons, in a particularity of their mentation.

- This particularity exists in everyone who possess a "soft and slippery 'something.' "

- This "soft and slippery 'something' " is a small 'law-conformable confusion.'

- This small 'law-conformable confusion' should play a part in the animation of other mentation functions.

- When, thanks to other actions, a "change of presence" occurs, which allows the center of gravity of the whole functioning of mentation to pass from its usual place to a different place, unexpected results occur.

- This "change of presence" naturally happens periodically.

- This small and slippery 'something' within the person plays a very small part in this "change of presence."

- The unexpected results are ridiculous to the point of absurdity.

absurd: "plainly illogical," 1550s, from French *absurde* (16c.), from Latin *absurdus* "out of tune, discordant," figuratively "incongruous, foolish, silly, senseless," from *ab-* "off, away from," here perhaps an intensive prefix, + *surdus* "dull, deaf, mute." The basic sense could be "out of tune."

We could theorize as to what this passage means. However, we leave it to the reader to do what they can. In our opinion, Gurdjieff is saying something meaningful here, that has to do with self-remembering.

other acts in its general functioning, immediately enables the center of gravity of the whole functioning, in which this slippery 'something' plays a very small part, to pass temporarily from its usual place to another place, owing to which there often obtains in the whole of this general functioning, unexpected results ridiculous to the point of absurdity."

He discharged the last words with such a shower of saliva that it was as if my face were exposed to the action of an "atomizer"—not of "Ersatz" production—invented by the Germans for dyeing material with aniline dyes.

This was more than I could endure, and without changing my squatting position, I flung myself at him, and my head, hitting him with full force in the pit of his stomach, immediately laid him out and made him as is said "lose consciousness."

I do not know and do not wish to know in what spirit the result will be formed in your mentation of the information about the extraordinary coincidence, in my opinion, of life circumstances, which I now intend to describe here, though for my mentation, this coincidence was excellent material for the assurance of the possibility of the fact that this event described by me, which occurred in my youth, proceeded not simply accidentally but was intentionally created by certain extraneous forces.

The point is that this dexterity was thoroughly taught me only a few days before this event by a Greek priest from Turkey, who, persecuted by Turks for his political convictions, had been compelled to flee from there, and having arrived in our town had been hired by my parents as a teacher for me of the modern Greek language.

I do not know on which data he based his political convictions and ideas, but I very well remember that in all the conversations of this Greek priest, even while explaining to me the difference between the words of exclamation

Atomizer

an "atomizer"—not of "Ersatz" production—invented by the Germans for dyeing material with aniline dyes.

Atomizers were used to apply aniline dyes. (Nowadays spray guns or airbrushes are used.) Because aniline dyes have low viscosity (much like water), they can be difficult to apply evenly with a brush or cloth without leaving darker streaks where the wet dye overlaps a section that has already begun to dry. An atomizer solves this by applying a fine, controlled mist that builds color gradually.

Gurdjieff's assertion that the atomizer was a German invention is open to debate. The invention of the atomizer (1887) is usually attributed to Dr. Allen DeVilbiss, a physician from Toledo, Ohio. Prior to his invention there were less sophisticated "atomizers." In 1858, Dr. Jean Sales-Girons, a Frenchman, created a portable "pulverizer" to treat respiratory issues. It was a heavy, hand-cranked device that forced medicinal water through a fine screen to create a mist.

The first aniline dye was discovered in 1856 by an English chemist named William Henry Perkin. Aniline, the base of Perkin's dye, was a derivative of coal tar. In the wake of Perkin's discovery, chemists realized they could manipulate coal tar to create almost any color.

Germans began using and manufacturing aniline dyes almost immediately after William Henry Perkin's discovery in 1856. This led to a commercial expansion that saw Germany take over the world market between 1861 and 1865. The atomizer that was first used for spraying aniline dyes was invented by Robert Koch, a German microbiologist.

Gurdjieff has much more to say about aniline dyes later in *The Tales*.[1]

As previously noted the German word "Ersatz" originally applied to units of the German army reserve that were regarded as inferior soldiers.

---

[1] *Beelzebub's Tales to His Grandson, p428*

The pit of the stomach

... hitting him with full force in the pit of his stomach, immediately laid him out and made him as is said "lose consciousness."

The pit of the stomach refers to the dent below the sternum which is the location of the solar plexus. A blow to the solar plexus could render someone unconscious, but is more likely to "wind" them. It can cause the diaphragm to go into a temporary spasm, temporarily preventing inhalation and exhalation.

Actual unconsciousness can happen when there is a "vaso-vagal" response. In this case, the impact stimulates the vagus nerve, which tells the heart to slow down and blood vessels to dilate. This leads to a sudden drop in blood pressure, depriving the brain of oxygen for a few seconds and causing the person to pass out.

Extraneous forces

that this event described by me, which occurred in my youth, proceeded not simply accidentally but was intentionally created by certain extraneous forces.

We presume this is an implication that fate took a hand in arranging this event. Gurdjieff notes that he was only taught how to head-butt someone in the solar plexus a few days before and was thus trying out the technique he had been taught for the first time.

Greek words of exclamation

... even while explaining to me the difference between the words of exclamation in ancient and in modern Greek, ...

As Gurdjieff suggests, there is a difference between ancient and modern Greek exclamations. We know about ancient Greek exclamations from the text of ancient Greek plays. In a few instances the sounds are the same, for example:

- Αχ! (Ach!): Used to express pain, longing, or relief.

- Ω! (O!): Used as a formal prefix to a name (like "O King!") or as a general "Oh!" of surprise.

- Ωχ! (Och!): A sound for surprise or "oh no."

In Ancient Greek, exclamations were often written to be performed in theater. They are more rhythmic and "melodic". Many sound strange to the modern ear because they include double vowels and unique breathy sounds. Here are some examples:

- Οἴμοι (Oimoi): The ultimate Ancient cry of "Woe is me!" Modern Greeks don't use this, but they use the root of it in the word for "lamenting" (oimogi).

- Αἰαῖ (Aiai): A high-pitched cry of grief common in Greek tragedies (like those by Sophocles or Euripides).

- Παπαῖ (Papai): Used to express sudden pain or astonishment. It's the ancient version of "Whoa!" or "Holy cow!"

- Ἄπαγε (Apage): Literally "Go away!" You might recognize this from the phrase "Apage Satana" (Begone, Satan).

Modern Greek contains some exclamations borrowed from other languages and, of course, changes with fashion. Such knowledge was clearly part of Gurdjieff's education.

in ancient and in modern Greek, there were indeed always very clearly discernible his dreams of getting as soon as possible to the island of Crete and there manifesting himself as befits a true patriot.

Well, then, on beholding the effect of my skill, I was, I must confess, extremely frightened, because, knowing nothing of any such reaction from a blow in that place, I quite thought I had killed him.

At the moment I was experiencing this fear, another boy, the cousin of him who had become the first victim of my so to say "skill in self-defense," seeing this, without a moment's pause, and obviously overcome with a feeling called "consanguinity," immediately leaped at me and with a full swing struck me in the face with his fist.

From this blow, I, as is said, "saw stars," and at the same time my mouth became as full as if it had been stuffed with the food necessary for the artificial fattening of a thousand chickens.

After a little time when both these strange sensations had calmed down within me, I then actually discovered that some foreign substance was in my mouth, and when I pulled it out with my fingers, it turned out to be nothing less than a tooth of large dimensions and strange form.

Seeing me staring at this extraordinary tooth, all the boys swarmed around me and also began to stare at it with great curiosity and in a strange silence.

By this time the boy who had been laid out flat recovered and, picking himself up, also began to stare at my tooth with the other boys, as if nothing had happened to him.

This strange tooth had seven shoots and at the end of each of them there stood out in relief a drop of blood, and through each separate drop there shone clearly and definitely one of the seven aspects of the manifestation of the white ray.

The island of Crete

...there were indeed always very clearly discernible his dreams of getting as soon as possible to the island of Crete and there manifesting himself as befits a true patriot.

The Greek War of Independence spanned a decade of the 19th century (1821–1830). Mainland Greece successfully achieved independence, but the Greek uprising in Crete was suppressed. Nevertheless throughout the rest of the 19th century revolution simmered. The most significant uprising began in 1866, quickly leading to the "Holocaust of Arkadi," when hundreds of Cretans chose to blow up their gunpowder stores, killing themselves and their attackers rather than surrender.

In 1868, the Ottoman Sultan issued the so-called "Organic Law," which granted Christians a degree of administrative participation in the government of Crete—but nothing more. Following the Russo-Turkish War (1877–1878), the Ottomans were forced (by The Pact of Halepa) to grant Crete extensive autonomy. A Christian governor was appointed, and Greek was recognized as an official language.

However, in 1889, Sultan Abdul Hamid II cracked down on Crete's freedoms. Local factional fighting had broken out on the island. Using this as an excuse, the Sultan sent 40,000 troops to Crete, declared martial law, and revoked The Pact of Halepa. This set the stage for an explosion of violence.

That would have been around the time that Gurdjieff was an adolescent, and the revoking of The Pact of Halepa was probably why his Greek tutor dreamed of joining the Greek patriots in Crete. Crete achieved a level of independence in 1897 when the Great Powers of the day (Britain, France, Russia, Italy) intervened. They forced the Sultan to withdraw all Ottoman troops from Crete. Crete finally achieved union with Greece in 1908.

Consanguinity

obviously overcome with a feeling called "consanguinity,"

consanguinity: "kinship by common descent," c. 1400, from Old French *consanguinité* and directly from Latin *consanguinitatem* (nominative *consanguinitas*), from *consanguineus* "of the same blood," from assimilated form of *com* "with, together" + *sanguineus* "of blood."

From this blow

From this blow, I, as is said, "saw stars," and at the same time my mouth became as full as if it had been stuffed with the food necessary for the artificial fattening of a thousand chickens.

The idiom "to see stars" describes the physical sensation of seeing flashing lights or spots of light in your vision, usually after a sudden physical trauma. The physical impact or pressure stimulates the primary visual cortex at the back of the brain or the retina in the eyes. Because these parts of the body only know how to communicate via visual signals, the brain interprets the physical jolt as "light," resulting in the flickering "stars."

A blow to the face will usually generate a rapid-fire sequence of sensory shocks that involve sight, sound, and a sudden, jarring shift in the internal map of where the body is in space. Among the sensory experiences are visual distortion, a heavy dull thud, that vibrates through the skull, a feeling of heat in the impact area, and a feeling of expansion—as though the injured area is growing. The entire face feels heavy and "thick."

This might be what Gurdjieff is describing when he writes: *my mouth became as full as if it had been stuffed with the food necessary for the artificial fattening of a thousand chickens.*

The fattening of a thousand chickens is a strange metaphor. Perhaps it implies that the blow engendered a powerful feeling of cowardice—an impulse of chicken-heartedness. When he calms down, he realizes that there is a dislodged tooth in his mouth.

Seven shoots

This strange tooth had seven shoots ...

In general teeth have few roots—two or three. In very rare instances, in individuals with specific genetic predispositions, molars have been found with as many as five to seven root fragments or branches, though these are often fused or rudimentary. However, teeth have roots, not shoots.

shoot: "young branch of a tree or plant," mid-15c., from the verb "shoot." Also "heavy, sudden rush of water; a river-fall or rapid," especially one through which a canoe or timber can "shoot" (1610s); "artificial channel for water running down" (1707); "conduit for coal, etc." (1844). In some senses influenced by or confused with "chute."

The white ray

... seven shoots and at the end of each of them there stood out in relief a drop of blood, and through each separate drop there shone clearly and definitely one of the seven aspects of the manifestation of the white ray.

Clearly this is metaphorical. For the first time in *The Tales* the Law of Seven is introduced. White light is composed of a continuous range of colors, and although the transition between these colors is fluid, they are traditionally categorized into the seven distinct bands of Red, Orange, Yellow, Green, Blue, Indigo, Violet. This can be clearly viewed when a white ray passes through a glass prism, and refraction splits the white ray into its various rainbow colors.

The blood and the seven colors may signify different branches of knowledge.

After this silence, unusual for us "young rascals," the usual hubbub broke out again, and in this hubbub it was decided to go immediately to the barber, a specialist in extracting teeth, and to ask him just why this tooth was like that.

So we all climbed down from the roof and went off to the barber's. And I, as the "hero of the day," stalked at the head of them all.

The barber, after a casual glance, said it was simply a "wisdom tooth" and that all those of the male sex have one like it, who until they first exclaim "papa" and "mama" are fed on milk exclusively from their own mother, and who on first sight are able to distinguish among many other faces the face of their own father.

As a result of the whole totality of the effects of this happening, at which time my poor "wisdom tooth" became a complete sacrifice, not only did my consciousness begin, from that time on, constantly absorbing, in connection with everything, the very essence of the essence of my deceased grandmother's behest—God bless her soul—but also in me at that time, because I did not go to a "qualified dentist" to have the cavity of this tooth of mine treated, which as a matter of fact I could not do because our home was too far from any contemporary center of culture, there began to ooze chronically from this cavity a "something" which—as it was only recently explained to me by a very famous meteorologist with whom I chanced to become, as is said, "bosom friends" owing to frequent meetings in the Parisian night restaurants of Montmartre—had the property of arousing an interest in, and a tendency to seek out the causes of the arising of every suspicious "actual fact"; and this property, not transmitted to my entirety by heredity, gradually and automatically led to my ultimately becoming a specialist

The barber

it was decided to go immediately to the barber, a specialist in extracting teeth, and to ask him just why this tooth was like that.

For much of history, among the general population, the barber served as a doctor of a kind with other duties aside from cutting hair and shaving beards. In medieval Europe, the Church played a pivotol role in establishing this profession. Monks were the original keepers of medical knowledge (for a while, in fact, of all knowledge) and they were required to maintain a tonsure (a shaved patch on top of their heads).

Monks could not "shed blood" due to religious decrees (notably the Council of Tours in 1163), so they delegated surgical tasks to their barbers, who were already on hand skilled with the use of razors. The medical tasks barber surgeons undertook included: bloodletting (puncturing a vein to "balance the humors"), amputations, and dentistry.

Stalked

And I, as the "hero of the day," stalked at the head of them all.

stalk: pursue stealthily. Middle English stalken, "walk cautiously or stealthily, step quietly and softly," from Old English -*stealcian*, as in *bestealcian* "to steal along, walk warily," from Proto-Germanic *stalkon*. The meaning "harass obsessively" is recorded by 1991.

This word choice is surprising. Gurdjieff "stalks" at the head of them, pursuing knowledge.

Wisdom tooth

The term "wisdom tooth" is a literal translation of older classical terms that associated the eruption of these teeth with the onset of adulthood and intellectual maturity. Hippocrates (c. 400 BC) referred to them as *sophronisteres*, derived from *sōphron*, meaning "prudent" or "self-controlled." The Romans later translated this as *dens sapientiae*, which literally means "tooth of wisdom." The phrase first appeared in English in the mid-17th century as "teeth of wisdom." It wasn't until the mid-19th century (around 1848) that the term was shortened to the modern "wisdom tooth."

The name is based entirely on the time of appearance. The third molars typically erupt between the ages of 17 and 25, marking the transition from childhood to adulthood.

So at the age depicted in the text, Gurdjieff was actually too young to have wisdom teeth.

The barber's opinion

The barber, after a casual glance, said it was simply a "wisdom tooth" and that all those of the male sex have one like it, who until they first exclaim "papa" and "mama" are fed on milk exclusively from their own mother, and who on first sight are able to distinguish among many other faces the face of their own father.

There is a great deal wrong with what the barber says. In general people have four wisdom teeth, not one. Not all men and women have wisdom teeth. In 10% to 35% of people, depending on geography, the teeth never form. Some studies suggest that females are slightly more likely than males to be missing wisdom teeth, but most women have them.

None of the other details given by the barber are correct. The possession of wisdom teeth is not dependent on being breast-fed as a baby or on recognizing the face of one's father.

Professional dentist

As Gurdjieff indicates, in the late 19th century, Armenia was in a state of transition regarding medical care. The modern profession of dentistry was just beginning to take root in major urban centers, but most dental care in rural areas relied on the traditional barber surgeon.

A very famous meteorologist

... as it was only recently explained to me by a very famous meteorologist with whom I chanced to become, as is said, "bosom friends" owing to frequent meetings in the Parisian night restaurants of Montmartre...

Etymologically, a meteorologist was originally someone who studied "lofty things" or "things high in the air." The word derives from the ancient Greek word *metéōros* (high in the air) and *logos* (treatise/discussion). When the concept was first popularized by Aristotle around 340 BC, the definition was far broader than just "weather forecasting." In the ancient world, there was no clear distinction between the atmosphere and outer space.

Therefore, a meteorologist was a philosopher who studied anything that occurred between the Earth's surface and the moon, including the weather, astronomy (shooting stars, comets, and the planets), geology (earthquakes and volcanoes) and other phenomena such as rainbows and halos around the sun. Early meteorologists were also astrologers.

We do not know exactly to whom Gurdjieff is referring, who expressed this opinion about the substance that oozed from Gurdjieff's cavity.

Montmartre

Montmartre is, at 130 meters, the highest hill in Paris. In ancient times it was a site for temples dedicated to Mars and Mercury. It was then called Mons Martis (the Mount of Mars).

As Christianity spread, the name was changed to Mons Martyrum. This refers to the martyrdom of Saint Denis, the first Bishop of Paris and the patron saint of France. Around 250 AD, Saint Denis was decapitated on the hill by the Romans.

According to legend, he picked up his head and walked several miles north to the spot where the Basilica of Saint-Denis now stands.

in the investigation of every suspicious phenomenon which, as it so often happened, came my way.

—

A chronic oozing

... there began to ooze chronically from this cavity a "something" which... had the property of arousing an interest in, and a tendency to seek out the causes of the arising of every suspicious "actual fact"; and this property, not transmitted to my entirety by heredity, gradually and automatically led to my ultimately becoming a specialist in the investigation of every suspicious phenomenon which, as it so often happened, came my way.

When a wisdom tooth is removed, the mouth immediately begins a complex biological repair process. The cavity will "ooze" for a short period. This is completely normal for the first 24 to 48 hours. The substance is a combination of blood and pink-colored saliva. After a few days, the socket may develop a yellowish or whitish appearance, which is a "wet scab" forming over the wound.

Gurdjieff is clearly not describing such substances. He is saying that something in the wisdom tooth incident caused Gurdjieff to become inquisitive about and investigate what he calls "suspicious phenomenon."

The reality is that many explanations that people believe about phenomena are simply repeated opinions about things they have never investigated. Gurdjieff became someone who did investigate.

This property newly formed in me after this event—when I, of course with the co-operation of our ALL-COMMON MASTER THE MERCILESS HEROPASS, that is the "flow of time," was transformed into the young man already depicted by me—became for me a real inextinguishable hearth, always burning, of consciousness.

The second of the mentioned vivifying factors, this time for the complete fusion of my dear grandmother's injunction with all the data constituting my general individuality, was the totality of impressions received from information I chanced to acquire concerning the event which took place here among us on Earth, showing the origin of that "principle" which, as it turned out according to the elucidations of Mr. Alan Kardec during an "absolutely secret" spiritualistic seance, subsequently became everywhere among beings similar to ourselves, arising and existing on all the other planets of our Great Universe, one of the chief "life principles."

The formulation in words of this new "all-universal principle of living" is as follows:

"If you go on a spree then go the whole hog including the postage."

As this "principle," now already universal, arose on that same planet on which you too arose and on which, moreover, you exist almost always on a bed of roses and frequently dance the fox trot, I consider I have no right to withhold from you the information known to me, elucidating certain details of the arising of just that universal principle.

Soon after the definite inculcation into my nature of the said new inherency, that is, the unaccountable striving to elucidate the real reasons for the arising of all sorts of "actual facts," on my first arrival in the heart of Russia,

Chapter VII

The Arousing of Thought 35-42

Alan Kardec

Gurdjieff deliberately misspells the name Allan Kardec as "Alan Kardec." He misspells other names at various places throughout *The Tales*. It is not clear why, but in every instance it is the name of someone of whom he is critical.

Allan Kardec was the pen name of the French educator, translator, and writer Hippolyte Léon Denizard Rivail (1804–1869), who became famous as the founder and "codifier" of Spiritism. Rivail did not choose this pen name randomly. According to his account, during a "communication with a spirit named Zéfiro," he was told that in a previous life, he had lived as a Druid in Gaul, and in that lifetime, his name was Allan Kardec.

In the mid-1850s, Rivail began investigating the phenomenon of "turning tables." Starting around 1852, it became a fashionable parlor activity for groups of people to sit around a table with their fingertips lightly touching its surface, waiting for it to move. The sitters joined hands or placed fingertips on a wooden table to form a "chain of energy." After a period of quiet concentration, the table would begin to shake, rotate, or tilt. When that happened, participants would ask questions. The "spirits" would supposedly answer them by tilting the table—for example, one tilt for "yes" and two for "no." To spell out words, someone would recite the alphabet, and the table would tip when the correct letter was reached.

Though initially skeptical of these séances, Rivail became convinced that the communications were originating from spirits. He adopted the pseudonym Allan Kardec to separate his Spiritist writings from his professional educational works.

He codified the Spiritist movement's principles through five foundational books, often called the Spiritist Codification. They are: *The Spirits' Book* (1857), *The Mediums' Book* (1861), *The Gospel According to Spiritism* (1864), *Heaven and Hell* (1865) and *The Genesis According to Spiritism* (1868).

His teachings embraced reincarnation, maintaining that spirits inhabit different bodies over multiple lifetimes in pursuit of intellectual and moral perfection. He asserted people could communicate with the deceased via "gifted" mediums. He also asserted that life exists on other planets and that there are other planes of existence.

His grave at the Père Lachaise Cemetery in Paris is one of the most visited. It features the inscription:

"To be born, to die, to be reborn again, and to progress constantly, such is the law."

A further note on Spiritism

The table turning craze was so widespread that it caught the attention of Michael Faraday, the famous physicist. In 1853, he conducted a series of rigorous experiments to determine if the table movements were caused by spirits, electricity, or "animal magnetism." To do so, he created an apparatus using layers of cardboard and glass rollers placed between the sitters' hands and the table. His experiments revealed that the table movement was caused by the participants' own muscles moving involuntarily. Because they expected or wanted the table to move, their bodies made tiny, subconscious movements that eventually gained enough momentum to shift the furniture.

When Faraday used an indicator (a small needle) that showed the sitters they were the ones pushing the table, the "supernatural" movements immediately stopped because the participants became consciously aware of their actions.

It seems then that whatever communication occurs in séances happen through the participants, perhaps unconsciously.

The "all-universal principle of living"

The formulation in words of this new "all-universal principle of living" is as follows:

"If you go on a spree then go the whole hog including the postage."

spree: "a lively frolic, rowdy drinking bout," 1804, slang or colloquial, earliest in Scottish dialect works, a word of uncertain origin. Perhaps an alteration of French *esprit* "lively wit," although early uses suggest the original pronunciation was as *spray*. According to Klein, Irish *spre* seems to be a loan-word from Old Norse *sprakr*. Watkins proposes a possible origin as an alteration of Scots *spreath* "cattle raid," from Gaelic *sprédh, spré*, "cattle; wealth," from Middle Irish *preit, preid*, "booty," ultimately from Latin *praeda* "plunder, booty."

Etymologists believe that "the whole hog" idiom developed from the act of buying an entire animal rather than just specific cuts. In the late 18th and early 19th centuries, "going the whole hog" meant you weren't just settling for the cheap parts or a few sausages—you were buying the entire carcass.

This is reflected in the work of British poet William Cowper in his 1779 poem *The Love of the World Reproved*. He tells a satirical story of Muslim theologians debating which part of a hog was "forbidden" to eat. Since they couldn't agree on which specific part was haram, they ended up eating the whole thing.

In 17th and 18th-century Ireland, a "hog" was a slang term for a shilling. If someone spent a "whole hog" on one item (like a single drink), they were being extravagant or "going all out" with their money.

The phrase gained massive popularity in the United States during the 1820s and 30s. It was frequently used in the context of Andrew Jackson's presidency. His supporters were called "Whole Hoggers" because they supported his policies completely, without compromise.

Postal systems have a long history rooted in the ancient need for rulers to maintain control over vast empires. The first truly sophisticated postal system was created c. 550 BCE in Persia, under Cyrus the Great. The Persians calculated how far a horse could run at full speed before tiring and built relay stations (called Chapar Khaneh) at those exact intervals along the Royal Road. Couriers would carry a message to a relay station, then immediately transfer the message to a fresh rider and horse. The message would travel without pause.

The Romans adopted a similar system. The word "post" comes from the Latin word *positus*, the past participle of *ponere* (meaning "to place" or "to set"). In Rome, it referred to the stations (the "placed" spots) where couriers and fresh horses were positioned.

A bed of roses

As this "principle," now already universal, arose on that same planet on which you too arose and on which, moreover, you exist almost always on a bed of roses...

The term "bed of roses" is an English idiom used to describe a life or situation that is easy, comfortable, and free from trouble.

In Ancient Rome, wealthy Romans were known to fill their mattresses with rose petals or scatter them inches deep on the floor during banquets. The Roman philosopher Seneca (1st Century AD) used the image to contrast luxury with hardship. In his writings, he noted that one does not learn how to endure suffering by lying on a "bed of roses." The idiom also took root in Renaissance poetry in its use by English poet and playwright Christopher Marlowe in his famous 1599 poem, "The Passionate Shepherd to His Love."

The fox trot

and on which, moreover, you exist almost always on a bed of roses and frequently dance the fox trot,

The fox trot is a classic ballroom dance that emerged in 1914 and ultimately became the most popular dance of the 20th century. However, it was considered rebellious and even scandalous when it first debuted.

The dance originated in New York City and was named after vaudeville performer Harry Fox. It is a smooth, progressive dance where couples travel counter-clockwise around the floor. Nowadays, it is characterized by long, flowing steps and a "Slow-Quick-Quick" or "Slow-Slow-Quick-Quick" rhythm.

To the Victorian-minded older generation of 1914, the foxtrot represented a breakdown of social morals. This was because of the physical proximity of the two dancers (the "closed hold") where the leader's right hand was placed firmly on the follower's back. To critics, this was "unseemly" and suggested a level of intimacy that should not happen in a public ballroom.

The dance also coincided with a shift in women's fashion. To perform the fox trot's long strides, women had to ditch their restrictive corsets and wear shorter skirts. This link between the dance and the "New Woman"—who was more independent and physically active—was abhorred by social conservatives.

the city of Moscow, where, finding nothing else for the satisfaction of my psychic needs, I occupied myself with the investigation of Russian legends and sayings, I once happened—whether accidentally or as a result of some objective sequence according to a law I do not know—to learn by the way the following:

Once upon a time a certain Russian, who in external appearance was to those around him a simple merchant, had to go from his provincial town on some business or other to this second capital of Russia, the city of Moscow, and his son, his favorite one—because he resembled only his mother—asked him to bring back a certain book.

When this great unconscious author of the "all-universal principle of living" arrived in Moscow, he together with a friend of his became—as was and still is usual there—"blind drunk" on genuine "Russian vodka."

And when these two inhabitants of this most great contemporary grouping of biped breathing creatures had drunk the proper number of glasses of this "Russian blessing" and were discussing what is called "public education," with which question it has long been customary always to begin one's conversation, then our merchant suddenly remembered by association his dear son's request, and decided to set off at once to a bookshop with his friend to buy the book.

In the shop, the merchant, looking through the book he had asked for and which the salesman handed him, asked its price.

The salesman replied that the book was sixty kopecks. Noticing that the price marked on the cover of the book was only forty-five kopecks, our merchant first began pondering in a strange manner, in general unusual for Russians, and afterwards, making a certain movement with his shoulders, straightening himself up almost like a pillar and throwing out his chest like an officer of the

Blind drunk

The *Oxford English Dictionary* traces the term "blind drunk" back to at least 1740. At that time it was a figurative description of someone who was so intoxicated they could "see no better than a blind man." It described the physical symptoms of heavy drinking—so intoxicated that one's senses, judgment, and physical coordination are severely impaired.

Later, in the U.S., the phrase became associated with the dangerous bootleg liquor of the 1920s. Illegal "moonshine" or bootleg spirits were often poorly distilled or intentionally "cut" with methanol (wood alcohol). When digesting this, formic acid is produced, which specifically attacks the optic nerve.

Russian vodka

Russian Finance Minister Sergei Witte introduced the State Vodka Monopoly in 1894 motivated in part by concerns over public health but also a desire for massive tax revenue. This eliminated the private distillers, who sold adulterated spirits, and ensured that the state received 100% of the profits. By the early 1900s, vodka revenue accounted for nearly one-third of the Russian Empire's entire budget.

The state established strict recipes, the most famous being "Moscow Special" (Moskovskaya Osobaya), which included small amounts of sodium bicarbonate and acetic acid to soften the taste. Also, charcoal filtration was introduced and this process absorbed "fusel oils" (unpleasant fermentation byproducts), resulting in a clear, odorless spirit that became the benchmark for "Russian quality."

At the time, vodka was rarely drunk alone. It was the centerpiece of the "Zakusochnyi Stol" (snack table), paired with salty and fatty foods like pickled cucumbers, herring, rye bread, and lard.

guards, said after a little pause, very quietly but with an intonation in his voice expressing great authority:

"But it is marked here forty-five kopecks. Why do you ask sixty?" Thereupon the salesman, making as is said the "oleaginous" face proper to all salesmen, replied that the book indeed cost only forty-five kopecks, but had to be sold at sixty because fifteen kopecks were added for postage.

After this reply to our Russian merchant who was perplexed by these two quite contradictory but obviously clearly reconcilable facts, it was visible that something began to proceed in him, and gazing up at the ceiling, he again pondered, this time like an English professor who has invented a capsule for castor oil, and then suddenly turned to his friend and delivered himself for the first time on Earth of the verbal formulation which, expressing in its essence an indubitable objective truth, has since assumed the character of a saying.

And he then put it to his friend as follows:

"Never mind, old fellow, we'll take the book. Anyway we're on a spree today, and 'if you go on a spree then go the whole hog including the postage.'"

As for me, unfortunately doomed, while still living, to experience the delights of "Hell," as soon as I had cognized all this, something very strange, that I have never experienced before or since, immediately began, and for a rather long time continued to proceed in me; it was as if all kinds of, as contemporary "Hivintzes" say, "competitive races" began to proceed in me between all the various-sourced associations and experiences usually occurring in me.

At the same time, in the whole region of my spine there began a strong almost unbearable itch, and a colic in the very center of my solar plexus, also unbearable, and all this, that is these dual, mutually stimulating sensations,

Oleaginous

... making as is said the "oleaginous" face proper to all salesmen, ...

This word comes from the Latin *oleaginus*, meaning "of the olive tree," referring to the oily and greasy properties of olive oil. It is used here figuratively to describe a salesman, implying someone who is slippery, insincere and employs excessive flattery.

A capsule for castor oil

... he again pondered, this time like an English professor who has invented a capsule for castor oil ...

Creating a capsule for castor oil turns out to be a highly specialized engineering task—although not one that an English Professor would be likely to concern himself with. Presumably Gurdjieff is hinting here at the laxative (purgative) properties of castor oil. The Russian merchant simply decides to purge himself of the problem rather than argue the point. And so he utters for the first time this memorable "all-universal principle of living."

Hivintzes

it was as if all kinds of, as contemporary "Hivintzes" say, "competitive races" began to proceed in me between all the various-sourced associations and experiences usually occurring in me.

Gurdjieff was unable to pronounce an English "h." The original Russian word was probably Khivintsy (Хивинцы). This word refers to the people of the Khanate of Khiva, a historical state in Central Asia (modern-day Uzbekistan and Turkmenistan).

The Khivintsy are part of a profound Central Asian equestrian culture where horses and racing have been central to life for over a thousand years. Horse races are a staple of festivals, weddings, and religious holidays. The races are typically long-distance endurance tests over open terrain, testing a horse's stamina and its rider's ability to navigate the harsh desert and steppe environment of the Khwarazm region.

They also play a sport called Kupkari (or Ulak-kupkari), where hundreds of riders on horseback compete to grab a goat carcass and carry it to a goal. While it involves "racing" to the finish line, it is more like a massive, mounted wrestling match.

Khiva was a major trade hub on the Silk Road and was famous for its "Heavenly Horses" (Argamaks). These horses were prized for being incredibly fast, lean, and possessing a "metallic" sheen on their coats.

Constate

This (page 38) is the first time that the word "constate" is used in the text of *The Tales*. The word means "to establish, or verify a fact." Gurdjieff uses the word repeatedly throughout the rest of *The Tales*.

constate: borrowed into English in the 18th century from the French verb *constater*. In French, *constater* means "to state as a fact, to certify, or to notice a reality." The French term is derived from the Latin *constat*, which is the third-person singular present indicative of the verb *constare*. *con-* (together/thoroughly) + *stare* (to stand).

It is a fundamental aspect of the Work that one needs to establish for oneself what is real.

The paragraph that spans pages 37 to 39

Starting on page 37, Gurdjieff writes a single long complex paragraph that ends on page 39. It takes some unpacking. We print the beginning and the end of this long paragraph below:

At the same time, in the whole region of my spine there began a strong almost unbearable ...

... a drunken state by a person quite alien to me—some merchant of "Muscovite brand."

Our summary is this:

As soon as Gurdjieff understood this universal principle, his mind became a chaotic mess of competing thoughts and memories, (competitive races). This mental chaos triggered intense physical pain—an unbearable itch along his spine and a sharp, "colicky" cramping in his solar plexus.

He says that his "I" turns his attention inward and then it, i.e. the attention, constated. So, his attention constated, not his "I".

His "I" is able to do this because it is the same "I". The word "same," as we learned from *Life Is Real Only Then, When 'I Am'*, is important because attention is defined as "the degree of blending of that which is the same in the impulses of observation and constatation in one totality's processes with that occurring in other totalities."[1]

So his "I" has observed the same thing going on in all three totalities: sensation (itchiness in his spine), colic in his solar plexus and the thought "when you go on a spree..." in his thinking centre. So his "I" is now this same I, powerful because the attention has blended together the same data from each separate centre.

So his "I" knows only because his attention knows it, i. e. has blended all of the same data in three centres together. The "I" is defined as a "relatively transferable arising..." so it is not permanent but can range or transfer on to any function or not. It can also hover (arise) over oneself without identifying with this or that particular instinct, feeling or thought.

This gave way to a deep, rare peace (which he compared to a high-level spiritual initiation.) In this calm state, his "I" observed this principle merging with the two established values within him (grandma's behest and the wisdom tooth) to create a new "substance" that settled into every atom of his body. He then realized that he was "fated" for the rest of his life to act in accordance with these three things. Before this, he had acted differently from others just by habit. But now he began to act with full consciousness and a sense of duty to "Great Nature."

[1] *Life Is Real Only Then, When 'I Am'* p147

after the lapse of some time suddenly were replaced by such a peaceful inner condition as I experienced in later life once only, when the ceremony of the great initiation into the Brotherhood of the "Originators of making butter from air" was performed over me; and later when "I," that is, this "something-unknown" of mine, which in ancient times one crank—called by those around him, as we now also call such persons, a "learned man"—defined as a "relatively transferable arising, depending on the quality of the functioning of thought, feeling, and organic automatism," and according to the definition of another also ancient and renowned learned man, the Arabian Malel-Lel, which definition by the way was in the course of time borrowed and repeated in a different way by a no less renowned and learned Greek, Xenophon, "the compound result of consciousness, subconsciousness, and instinct"; so when this same "I" in this condition turned my dazed attention inside myself, then firstly it very clearly constated that everything, even to each single word, elucidating this quotation that has become an "all-universal life principle" became transformed in me into some special cosmic substance, and merging with the data already crystallized in me long before from the behest of my deceased grandmother, changed these data into a "something" and this "something" flowing everywhere through my entirety settled forever in each atom composing this entirety of mine, and secondly, this my ill-fated "I" there and then definitely felt and, with an impulse of submission, became conscious of this, for me, sad fact, that already from that moment I should willy-nilly have to manifest myself always and in everything without exception, according to this inherency formed in me, not in accordance with the laws of heredity, nor even by the influence of surrounding circumstances, but arising in my entirety

Making butter from air

> ... the ceremony of the great initiation into the Brotherhood of the "Originators of making butter from air" was performed over me; ...

Metaphorically, "making butter from air" might describe the act of creating something valuable or substantial from seemingly nothing. We were unable to find any reference to any such Brotherhood. We are unsure as to what Gurdjieff is trying to convey.

The Arabian Malel-Lel

> ... according to the definition of another also ancient and renowned learned man, the Arabian Malel-Lel, ...

The term "Arabia" first emerged over 2,800 years ago, appearing first in the records of ancient Middle Eastern empires to describe the people and lands to their west and south. Its use evolved from a vague label for "desert dwellers" to a formal name for the specific geographic Arabian peninsula.

In that historical timeframe the name "Malel" (or variants like "Malel-lel") most likely relates to a specific phonetic rendering of a local Semitic title. The name "Maleleel" would be a Greek/Latin variation of the Hebrew Mahalalel—a name that appears in the lineage of the patriarchs (he was the grandfather of Enoch). But that was a long long time before the word "Arabia" existed.

The name could mean "The Shining One of God" or "Praise of God." Helel (the root H-L-L) was used throughout the Middle East to describe the Morning Star. In ancient North Arabian scripts, the word for king is "Malik." Malel-lel could be a phonetic transcription of a title like "Malik-al-..." (King of...). Despite a long research effort, we found no individual in history with the name Malel-Lel.

Xenophon

> ... which definition by the way was in the course of time borrowed and repeated in a different way by a no less renowned and learned Greek, Xenophon, ...

Xenophon (c. 430–354 BCE) was a multi-faceted Greek figure who excelled as a soldier, historian, and philosopher. He was a student of Socrates, but he is also remembered for his daring military leadership and for writing the world's first first-person military memoir.

As a young man, he was part of the intellectual circle surrounding Socrates. Unlike Plato, who focused on abstract metaphysics, Xenophon's interest in Socratic thought leaned toward practical ethics and leadership.

His "Socratic works" (like *Memorabilia*) provide a crucial alternative perspective to Plato. Xenophon portrays Socrates as a practical moral teacher concerned with civic duty and self-control. He pioneered the "biographical novel" with *Cyropaedia* (*The Education of Cyrus*), which explores the qualities of an ideal ruler and influenced political thinkers for centuries.

under the influence of three external accidental causes, having nothing in common, namely: thanks in the first place to the behest of a person who had become, without the slightest desire on my part, a passive cause of the cause of my arising; secondly, on account of a tooth of mine knocked out by some ragamuffin of a boy, mainly on account of somebody else's "slobberiness"; and thirdly, thanks to the verbal formulation delivered in a drunken state by a person quite alien to me—some merchant of "Muscovite brand."

If before my acquaintance with this "all-universal principle of living" I had actualized all manifestations differently from other biped animals similar to me, arising and vegetating with me on one and the same planet, then I did so automatically, and sometimes only half consciously, but after this event I began to do so consciously and moreover with an instinctive sensation of the two blended impulses of self-satisfaction and self-cognizance in correctly and honorably fulfilling my duty to Great Nature.

It must even be emphasized that although even before this event I already did everything not as others did, yet my manifestations were hardly thrust before the eyes of my fellow countrymen around me, but from the moment when the essence of this principle of living was assimilated in my nature, then on the one hand all my manifestations, those intentional for any aim and also those simply, as is said, "occurring out of sheer idleness," acquired vivifyingness and began to assist in the formation of "corns" on the organs of perception of every creature similar to me without exception who directed his attention directly or indirectly toward my actions, and on the other hand, I myself began to carry out all these actions of mine in accordance with the injunctions of my deceased grandmother to the utmost possible limits; and the practice was automatically acquired in me on beginning anything new

Ragamuffin

... a tooth of mine knocked out by some ragamuffin of a boy, mainly on account of somebody else's "slobberiness"; ...

ragamuffin: mid-14c., "demon;" late 14c., "a ragged lout," also in surnames (Isabella Ragamuffyn, 1344), from Middle English *raggi* "ragged" + "fanciful ending" [OED 1989], or perhaps the second element is Middle Dutch *muffe* "mitten." As Johnson has it, "From rag and I know not what else." Ragged was used to describe the devil from c. 1300 in reference to his "shaggy" appearance. *Raggeman* (late 13c. as a surname, presumably "one who goes about in tattered clothes") was used by Langland as the name of a demon (late 14c.), and compare Old French *Ragamoffyn*, name of a demon in a mystery play. The specific sense of "dirty, disreputable boy" is attested by 1580s. Also compare *ragabash* "idle, worthless fellow" (c. 1600).

slobber: late 14c., *sloberen*, "dribble from the mouth," probably of imitative origin; compare Frisian *slobberje* "to slurp," Middle Low German *slubberen* "slurp," Middle Dutch *overslubberen* "wade through a ditch." Related: slobbered; slobbering. As noun from c. 1400 as "mud, slime," 1755 as "saliva."

Muscovite brand

... by a person quite alien to me—some merchant of "Muscovite brand."

First consider the word "brand." It has the following etymology:

brand: Old English *brand, brond* "fire, flame, destruction by fire; firebrand, piece of burning wood, torch," and (poetic) "sword," from Proto-Germanic *brandaz* "a burning" (source also of Old Norse *brandr*, Old High German *brant*, Old Frisian *brond* "firebrand; blade of a sword," German *brand* "fire"). The meaning "iron instrument for branding" is from 1828. The meaning "mark made by a hot iron" (1550s), especially on a cask, etc., to identify the maker or quality of its contents, had broadened by 1827 to include marks made in other ways, then to "a particular make of goods" (1854). Brand-name is from 1889; brand-loyalty from 1961. Old French *brand, brant,* Italian *brando* "sword" are from Germanic.

We might be inclined to think that "Muscovite" simply means an inhabitant of Moscow, except that this merchant, as previously stated in the text, was not from Moscow at all, but from the Russian provinces. This is reinforced by the word "brand" implying that the merchant was fundamentally (i.e. branded) a Muscovite. The word "Muscovite" has several possible implications:

1. In literature and history, "Muscovite" evokes a specific aesthetic of pre-Petrine (before Peter the Great) Russia.It suggests stasis, religious orthodoxy, and ancient tradition. To call something "Muscovite" in a literary sense is to call it heavy, ornate, and steeped in a medieval past.

2. Historically, "Muscovite" was used by Western Europeans to distinguish the people of the Moscow-centered state from "Europeans." It suggests a culture that is inherently alien, Asiatic, or semi-Oriental, rather than Western. So calling someone a Muscovite instead of a Russian, may imply that the person belongs to a tradition of "Eastern despotism" that is fundamentally incompatible with Western liberal values.

3. In contemporary Eastern European discourse (particularly in Ukraine, Poland, and the Baltic states), the term is sometimes used to strip away the "All-Russian" identity and frame the Russian state as merely the "Muscovite Tsardom"—suggesting an expansionist power occupying territories that do not belong to it. Because Moscow was the engine of the unification of Russian lands, "Muscovite" often carries the weight of unrelenting central power. Thus it may imply a "center-of-the-universe" mentality where the periphery exists only to serve the capital.

4. Due to the climate of Moscow and the historical reputation of its rulers (such as Ivan the Terrible), the word has developed a figurative association with severity. A "Muscovite" temperament is often depicted as stoic,

cold, calculating, and perhaps slightly ruthless. It suggests a person hardened by a harsh environment and an even harsher political system.

5. In early modern diplomatic texts, "The Muscovite" was often used as a title for the Tsar when Western monarchs wanted to subtly insult him by denying him the title of "Emperor" or "King of all the Russias."

Our view is that Gurdjieff intends us to take the first of these different implications of "Muscovite."

Corns

... began to assist in the formation of "corns" on the organs of perception of every creature similar to me without exception ...

Corns do not normally form on the organs of perception, so we can assume this is a metaphor. But we will probably know that from the many mentions by Gurdjieff of "corns" in the Work literature. For example:

And what seems to be positive in the emotional states experienced by people in ordinary waking state can go sour and turn into negativity with just a little pressure on one of what Gurdjieff called our "corns"—sensitive psychological issues and images which are generally founded on pride or vanity.[1]

Biologically, a corn is the result of a process where the skin's outer layer (the stratum corneum) thickens in response to chronic mechanical stress. They are frequent on toes and the sole of the foot, due to the constant pressure of footwear, but can develop in other areas of the body where there is repetitive friction or pressure.

Because of frequent friction, the body detects potential tissue damage. To prevent an open ulcer or blister, the skin accelerates the production of keratin, a tough, fibrous protein. The keratinized cells "pile up" into a dense, conical shape that points inward, pressing into the deeper, nerve-rich layers of the dermis. This is why they are often painful, particularly if subjected to pressure.

[1] *The Gurdjieff Work by Kathleen Riordan Speeth p46*

Metaphorically, the foot symbolizes personality and corns symbolizes sensitive areas of personality that Gurdjieff was adept at discovering and pressing down on.

So the paragraph:

> ... on the one hand all my manifestations, those intentional for any aim and also those simply, as is said, "occurring out of sheer idleness," acquired vivifyingness and began to assist in the formation of "corns" on the organs of perception of every creature similar to me without exception who directed his attention directly or indirectly toward my actions, and on the other hand, I myself began to carry out all these actions of mine in accordance with the injunctions of my deceased grandmother ...

... states that Gurdjieff's manifestations became energized and irritated everyone around him and, as suggested by his grandmother, he didn't do as others do.

and also at any change, of course on a large scale, always to utter silently or aloud:

"If you go on a spree then go the whole hog including the postage."

And now, for instance, in the present case also, since, owing to causes not dependent on me, but flowing from the strange and accidental circumstances of my life, I happen to be writing books, I am compelled to do this also in accordance with that same principle which has gradually become definite through various extraordinary combinations created by life itself, and which has blended with each atom of my entirety.

This psycho-organic principle of mine I shall this time begin to actualize not by following the practice of all writers, established from the remote past down to the present, of taking as the theme of their various writings the events which have supposedly taken place, or are taking place, on Earth, but shall take instead as the scale of events for my writings—the whole Universe. Thus in the present case also, "If you take then take!"—that is to say, "If you go on a spree then go the whole hog including the postage."

Any writer can write within the scale of the Earth, but I am not any writer.

Can I confine myself merely to this, in the objective sense, "paltry Earth" of ours? To do this, that is to say, to take for my writings the same themes as in general other writers do, I must not, even if only because what our learned spirits affirm might suddenly indeed prove true; and my grandmother might learn of this; and do you understand what might happen to her, to my dear beloved grandmother? Would she not turn in her grave, not once, as is usually said, but—as I understand her, especially now when I can already quite "skillfully" enter into the position of another—she would turn so many

The whole Universe

This psycho-organic principle of mine I shall this time begin to actualize not by following the practice of all writers, established from the remote past down to the present, of taking as the theme of their various writings the events which have supposedly taken place, or are taking place, on Earth, but shall take instead as the scale of events for my writings—the whole Universe.

True to his word, Gurdjieff does indeed write about the whole universe and he does so from multiple perspectives. It could also be said that he chooses to touch on many separate topics that would be unlikely to be brought togther in any book other than an encyclopedia.

times that she would almost be transformed into an "Irish weathercock."

Please, reader, do not worry ... I shall of course also write of the Earth, but with such an impartial attitude that this comparatively small planet itself and also everything on it shall correspond to that place which in fact it occupies and which, even according to your own sane logic, arrived at thanks of course to my guidance, it must occupy in our Great Universe.

I must, of course, also make the various what are called "heroes" of these writings of mine not such types as those which in general the writers of all ranks and epochs on Earth have drawn and exalted, that is to say, types such as any Tom, Dick, or Harry, who arise through a misunderstanding, and who fail to acquire during the process of their formation up to what is called "responsible life," anything at all which it is proper for an arising in the image of God, that is to say a man, to have, and who progressively develop in themselves to their last breath only such various charms as for instance: "lasciviousness," "slobberiness," "amorousness," "maliciousness," "chickenheartedness," "enviousness," and similar vices unworthy of man.

I intend to introduce in my writings heroes of such type as everybody must, as is said, "willy-nilly" sense with his whole being as real, and about whom in every reader data must inevitably be crystallized for the notion that they are indeed "somebody" and not merely "just anybody."

During the last weeks, while lying in bed, my body quite sick, I mentally drafted a summary of my future writings and thought out the form and sequence of their exposition, and I decided to make the chief hero of the first series of my writings ... do you know whom? ... the Great Beelzebub Himself—even in spite of the fact

The Irish weathercock

... and do you understand what might happen to her, to my dear beloved grandmother? Would she not turn in her grave, not once, as is usually said, but—as I understand her, especially now when I can already quite "skillfully" enter into the position of another—she would turn so many times that she would almost be transformed into an "Irish weathercock."

The weathercock Gurdjieff is probably referencing is the Salmon of Shandon, which perches on top of the 170-foot Shandon Bells tower of St. Anne's Church, Cork. It is, of course, not exactly a weathercock, but a 13-foot-long "weatherfish," the most famous weather vane in Ireland. The fish is, of course, a potent Christan symbol.

Fig 7. *The Irish weathercock.*

Heroes of such type...

I must, of course, also make the various what are called "heroes" of these writings of mine not such types as those which in general the writers of all ranks and epochs on Earth have drawn and exalted, ...

In English literature, there are several types or categories of hero:

- The **warrior hero**, embodying the values of a warrior. Think Achilles or Boewolf in classical literature. Modern day versions are comicbook heroes like Batman, Spiderman et al. Often they have to fight aginast some major weakness to protect their community.

- The **gallant knight** (a chivalric hero) emerged in early English romances derived from Arthurian legend. This hero is a blend of power and refined conduct. They are generally governed by some "code of chivalry"—loyalty, courtesy (toward women), and a degree of religious piety. They struggle against temptation.

- The **tragic hero** is typified by many Shakespearean characters. They are noble, but possessed of a tragic flaw that leads to an inner struggle that inevitably causes their downfall.

- The **outcast hero** (the Byronic Hero) is moody, cynical, highly intelligent, and emotionally "wounded." Good examples are Heathcliff in *Wuthering Heights* or Mr. Rochester in *Jane Eyre*. They are social outcasts who reject conventional morality, and tend to brood over some "secret" past.

- The **anti-hero** (or everyman hero) is ordinary, rather than noble. They struggle with everyday life and societal pressures. They may lack heroic qualities like courage or idealism. They may be dishonest, or even passive, yet they command the reader's attention.

The heroes of *The Tales* do not conform to such literary "heroic models." All of them, particularly the anti-hero, *fail to acquire during the process of their formation up to what is called "responsible life," anything at all which it is proper for an arising in the image of God.*

Beelzebub

... the Great Beelzebub Himself—even in spite of the fact that this choice of mine might from the very beginning evoke in the mentation of most of my readers such mental associations as must engender in them all kinds of automatic contradictory impulses ...

The associations that arise in the reader's mind will depend entirely on the various sources which engendered them. However, it is very likely that the automatic picture engendered by these associations will be very negative.

Beelzebub is a synonym for the Devil. Etymologically, the name came from the name of a Canaanite deity Ba'al Zebul, where *Ba'al* meant "Lord" and *Zebul* implied "Height," or "Exalted Dwelling."

Ba'al Zebub (similar but not the same) appears in the Old Testament (2 Kings 1). It appears that the ancient Israelites intentionally changed the last syllable to mock the foreign god—Zebub being the Hebrew word for "Fly." Ba'al Zebub was thus "Lord of the Flies." (From where William Golding got the title for his famous book *Lord of the Flies*.)

In the Greek New Testament and in Rabbinical literature, the name often appears as Beelzebul or Beelzeboul. This form of the name served as a dark pun in Aramaic and Hebrew—*Zebel*: meaning "dung"—hence "Lord of the Dungheap."

By the time of Jesus, the name Beelzebub had been thoroughly "demonized." It was used by the Pharisees as a title for the "Prince of Demons" (Matthew 12:24).

In Dante's *Inferno* (1320) Beelzebub is not a separate character from the ruler of Hell; rather, Beelzebub is one of the various names Dante uses for Satan.

In John Milton's *Paradise Lost* (1667), Milton depicts Beelzebub as Satan's second-in-command, arguably the most important character in Hell after the Devil himself. He is not a monster, but a fallen angel of immense majesty and intellect. While Satan is the fiery, ambitious leader, Beelzebub is the pragmatic counselor.

In various occult and theological traditions, Beelzebub was not just a common angel but a high-ranking member of the celestial hierarchy. In many Catholic demonology traditions (such as the *Admirable History* by Sébastien Michaëlis), Beelzebub was a Seraph, which is the highest order of angels, who had served under the Archangel Gabriel.

Most traditions that treat him as a separate entity from Satan place him at the very center of the war in Heaven. He is often depicted as the first angel to join Satan's rebellion. Because of his high status and powerful intellect, he became the Chief Lieutenant of the rebel army.

Gurdjieff never mentions Satan in *The Tales*, preferring the name Lucifer. Gurdjieff's Beelzebub is distinct from Lucifer and was personally responsible for the revolution in Heaven, which led to his exile.

Lucifer

"Lucifer" is not a name in that originates from biblical texts. It comes from the Latin *lucifer*, which literally means "light-bringer" (*lux* "light" + *ferre* "to bear"). As such, in the Roman world it was the name for the planet Venus, which appears as the "Morning Star" just before sunrise. In the Hebrew Bible (Isaiah 14:12), the title is Helel ben Shahar, meaning "shining one, son of the morning."

So Lucifer's "origin story" as a fallen angel follows a similar path to the demonization of Beelzebub. The passage in Isaiah 14 was originally a taunt directed at a human king of Babylon, comparing his political downfall to a star falling from the sky.

Early Church Fathers began to interpret this passage metaphorically. They linked the "falling star" in Isaiah to Jesus' statement in the New Testament: "I saw Satan fall like lightning from heaven" (Luke 10:18). This had the effect of merging the two figures, creating the modern "Lucifer": God's most beautiful and highest-ranking archangel who, fueled by pride, led a rebellion against the Creator and was cast down to become Satan (the "Adversary").

Gurdjieff's Lucifer is such a human adversary.

that this choice of mine might from the very beginning evoke in the mentation of most of my readers such mental associations as must engender in them all kinds of automatic contradictory impulses from the action of that totality of data infallibly formed in the psyche of people owing to all the established abnormal conditions of our external life, which data are in general crystallized in people owing to the famous what is called "religious morality" existing and rooted in their life, and in them, consequently, there must inevitably be formed data for an inexplicable hostility towards me personally.

Abnormal conditions

This is the first instance in *The Tales* where Gurdjieff states that the modern conditions of life are abnormal.

Religious morality

morality: late 14c., *moralite*, "moral qualities, virtuous conduct or thought," from Old French *moralite* (Modern French *moralité*) "moral (of a story); moral instruction; morals, moral character" (13c.) and directly from Late Latin *moralitatem* (nominative *moralitas*) "manner, character," from Latin *moralis* "of manners or morals; moral" (see moral (adj.)). Meaning "doctrine or system of ethical duties" is from mid-15c. Meaning "goodness, characteristic of being moral, virtuousness" is attested from 1590s.

In general culturally accepted morality derives from religious scripture:

- Judaism: from The Torah
- Christianity: from The Gospel / New Testament
- Islam: from The Quran / Sharia.
- Buddhism: from The Five Precepts and The Eightfold Path
- Hinduism: from The Dharma

Those who adhere to any of the first three of these will naturally feel a kind of animosity to anyone who champions a notorious fallen angel.

But do you know what, reader?

In case you decide, despite this Warning, to risk continuing to familiarize yourself with my further writings, and you try to absorb them always with an impulse of impartiality and to understand the very essence of the questions I have decided to elucidate, and in view also of the particularity inherent in the human psyche, that there can be no opposition to the perception of good only exclusively when so to say a "contact of mutual frankness and confidence" is established, I now still wish to make a sincere confession to you about the associations arisen within me which as a result have precipitated in the corresponding sphere of my consciousness the data which have prompted the whole of my individuality to select as the chief hero for my writings just such an individual as is presented before your inner eyes by this same Mr. Beelzebub.

This I did, not without cunning. My cunning lies simply in the logical supposition that if I show him this attention he infallibly—as I already cannot doubt any more—has to show himself grateful and help me by all means in his command in my intended writings.

Although Mr. Beelzebub is made, as is said, "of a different grain," yet, since He also can think, and, what

CHAPTER VIII

The Arousing of Thought 42-50

Another particularity of the human psyche

> ... and you try to absorb them always with an impulse of
> impartiality and to understand the very essence of the
> questions I have decided to elucidate, and in view also of the
> particularity inherent in the human psyche, that there can
> be no opposition to the perception of good only exclusively
> when so to say a "contact of mutual frankness and confid-
> ence" is established, ...

The reader may read through this paragraph without
considering its meaning. Note that it states that the reader will
be rewarded if he reads with an impulse of impartiality. This
will, of course, require effort.

Gurdjieff's cunning

> My cunning lies simply in the logical supposition that if I
> show him this attention he infallibly—as I already cannot
> doubt any more—has to show himself grateful and help me
> by all means in his command in my intended writings.

Whether this is cunning or not, is debateable. It is as
Gurdjieff says, a logical supposition and thus it may not be
true. Beelzebub may have no inclination to help out. No pact
has been made.

Of a different grain

This is a wordworking idiom. The "grain" refers to the
longitudinal arrangement of wood fibers. Different varieties
of wood have different grains and may be worked differently.
The transition from a carpentry term to a metaphor for
character and behavior happened in the 16th century.

is most important, has—as I long ago learned, thanks to the treatise of the famous Catholic monk, Brother Foolon—a curly tail, then I, being thoroughly convinced from experience that curls are never natural but can be obtained only from various intentional manipulations, conclude, according to the "sane-logic" of hieromancy formed in my consciousness from reading books, that Mr. Beelzebub also must possess a good share of vanity, and will therefore find it extremely inconvenient not to help one who is going to advertise His name.

It is not for nothing that our renowned and incomparable teacher, Mullah Nassr Eddin, frequently says:

"Without greasing the palm not only is it impossible to live anywhere tolerably but even to breathe."

And another also terrestrial sage, who has become such, thanks to the crass stupidity of people, named Till Eulenspiegel, has expressed the same in the following words:

"If you don't grease the wheels the cart won't go."

Knowing these and many other sayings of popular wisdom formed by centuries in the collective life of people, I have decided to "grease the palm" precisely of Mr. Beelzebub, who, as everyone understands, has possibilities and knowledge enough and to spare for everything.

Enough, old fellow! All joking even philosophical joking aside, you, it seems, thanks to all these deviations, have transgressed one of the chief principles elaborated in you and put in the basis of a system planned previously for introducing your dreams into life by means of such a new profession, which principle consists in this, always to remember and take into account the fact of the weakening of the functioning of the mentation of the contemporary reader and not to fatigue him with the perception of numerous ideas over a short time.

Moreover, when I asked one of the people always around me who are "eager to enter Paradise without fail

Brother Foolon

... what is most important, has—as I long ago learned, thanks to the treatise of the famous Catholic monk, Brother Foolon—a curly tail, ...

There is no famous Catholic monk with the name Foolon. There were several monks, friars and religious authors that produced treatises on the Devil. The most famous was St. Thomas Aquinas, who describes the Devil in his works *Summa Theologiae* and *De Malo*. However in both works he asserts that the Devil does not have a corporeal body, but is pure spirit.

The supposed "curly" or "pointed" tail that the Devil possesses is an invention of medieval art, combined with European folklore. Most likely such a representation of the devil's tail derives from the Greek god Pan or the satyr, both of which were half man/half goat.

The name Foolon is probably a Gurdjieffian invention. The Greek suffix *on* can mean "that which," so Foolon could mean someone who is a fool.

The "sane logic" of hieromancy

... then I, being thoroughly convinced from experience that curls are never natural but can be obtained only from various intentional manipulations, conclude, according to the "sane-logic" of hieromancy formed in my consciousness from reading books, ...

Curls are indeed natural, whether in respect of curly hair, where the shape of the hair follicle determines whether the hair curls, or in the case of animal tales where dogs, pigs and cats can all have curly tails.

Hieromancy is a form of divination performed by studying sacred objects or the various items used in a religious sacrifice. The term covers a category of divination practices that involve the physical remnants of a ritual which are "read" to reveal the future or "the will of the gods."

Etymologically, the word is from the Ancient Greek roots: h*ieros*, meaning "sacred" or "holy" and m*anteia* meaning "prophecy" or "divination." Historically, the practice was common in ancient Greece, Rome, and Mesopotamia. The common forms were:

- The study of the entrails of sacrificed animals.
- The study of the liver of sacrificed animals.
- Observing how sacrificial fire consumed an offering.
- Interpreting the movement and shape of the smoke rising from the altar.

He writes *formed in my consciousness from reading books*, which knowledge is, of course, not reliable knowledge at all.

Beelzebub's vanity

Mr. Beelzebub also must possess a good share of vanity, and will therefore find it extremely inconvenient not to help one who is going to advertise His name.

Beelzebub, as generally depicted in religious literature, certainly does possess "vanity" but if so he is only likely to help Gurdjieff if Gurdjieff paints a picture of him that he enjoys and finds subjectively flattering. This could indeed be the case, but we have no way of knowing whether it is.

All joking aside

All joking even philosophical joking aside, you, it seems, thanks to all these deviations, have transgressed one of the chief principles elaborated in you and put in the basis of a system planned previously for introducing your dreams into life by means of such a new profession, which principle consists in this, always to remember and take into account the fact of the weakening of the functioning of the mentation of the contemporary reader and not to fatigue him with the perception of numerous ideas over a short time.

Gurdjieff is admonishing himself here, confessing that his previous narrative about pleasing the Devil is merely in jest and violates one of the chief principles put into his writing activities—to allow for the weakness of the psyche of the reader and not introduce too many ideas within a short space of time.

To enter paradise without fail

... eager to enter Paradise without fail with their boots on ...

This is a criticism of some of his pupils. It is impossible to "enter paradise with one's boots on." In Christian symbolism footwear symbolizes personality (the point of contact with life). Boots or galoshes signify a strong personality that needs to be struggled with and tamed.

with their boots on," to read aloud straight through all that I have written in this introductory chapter, what is called my "I"—of course, with the participation of all the definite data formed in my original psyche during my past years, which data gave me among other things understanding of the psyche of creatures of different type but similar to me—constated and cognized with certainty that in the entirety of every reader without exception there must inevitably, thanks to this first chapter alone, arise a "something" automatically engendering definite unfriendliness towards me personally.

To tell the truth, it is not this which is now chiefly worrying me, but the fact that at the end of this reading I also constated that in the sum total of everything expounded in this chapter, the whole of my entirety in which the aforesaid "I" plays a very small part, manifested itself quite contrary to one of the fundamental commandments of that All-Common Teacher whom I particularly esteem, Mullah Nassr Eddin, and which he formulated in the words: "Never poke your stick into a hornets' nest."

The agitation which pervaded the whole system affecting my feelings, and which resulted from cognizing that in the reader there must necessarily arise an unfriendly feeling towards me, at once quieted down as soon as I remembered the ancient Russian proverb which states: "There is no offense which with time will not blow over."

But the agitation which arose in my system from realizing my negligence in obeying the commandment of Mullah Nassr Eddin, not only now seriously troubles me, but a very strange process, which began in both of my recently discovered "souls" and which assumed the form of an unusual itching immediately I understood this, began progressively to increase until it now evokes and produces an almost intolerable pain in the region a little below the

Engendering definite unfriendliness

... constated and cognized with certainty that in the entirety of every reader without exception there must inevitably, thanks to this first chapter alone, arise a "something" automatically engendering definite unfriendliness towards me personally.

Typically, the first-time reader of *The Tales* finds the writing style difficult to grapple with and frequently, the meaning of the text difficult to discern. At first blush it is off-putting and, naturally, the reader is very likely to be critical of the author for this. The level of reading effort the book demands is far greater than expected—even for the enthusiastic reader.

The whole of my entirety

... I also constated that in the sum total of everything expounded in this chapter, the whole of my entirety in which the aforesaid "I" plays a very small part, manifested itself quite contrary to one of the fundamental commandments of that All-Common Teacher ...

Gurdjieff confesses that his behavior is contrary to Mullah Nassr Eddin's advice: "Never poke your stick into a hornets' nest." However he realizes that the offense he has caused the reader will eventually blow over with time—as indeed it will in the experience of most readers.

An almost intolerable pain

Gurdjieff notes that his realization that he ignored Mullah Nassr Eddin's advice gave rise to an increasing "itching" producing an almost intolerable pain to the right and below his solar plexus (possibly in the liver or small intestine). But this ceases when he remembers another fragment of life wisdom concerning Karapet of Tiflis.

right half of my already, without this, overexercised "solar plexus."

Wait! Wait! ... This process, it seems, is also ceasing, and in all the depths of my consciousness, and let us meanwhile say "even beneath my subconsciousness," there already begins to arise everything requisite for the complete assurance that it will entirely cease, because I have remembered another fragment of life wisdom, the thought of which led my mentation to the reflection that if I indeed acted against the advice of the highly esteemed Mullah Nassr Eddin, I nevertheless acted without premeditation according to the principle of that extremely sympathetic—not so well known everywhere on earth, but never forgotten by all who have once met him—that precious jewel, Karapet of Tiflis.

It can't be helped .... Now that this introductory chapter of mine has turned out to be so long, it will not matter if I lengthen it a little more to tell you also about this extremely sympathetic Karapet of Tiflis.

First of all I must state that twenty or twenty-five years ago, the Tiflis railway station had a "steam whistle."

It was blown every morning to wake the railway workers and station hands, and as the Tiflis station stood on a hill, this whistle was heard almost all over the town and woke up not only the railway workers, but the inhabitants of the town of Tiflis itself.

The Tiflis local government, as I recall it, even entered into a correspondence with the railway authorities about the disturbance of the morning sleep of the peaceful citizens.

To release the steam into the whistle every morning was the job of this same Karapet who was employed in the station.

So when he would come in the morning to the rope with which he released the steam for the whistle, he

That precious jewel, Karapet of Tiflis

To refer to Karapet as a "precious jewel" is a considerable compliment. In the light of the story Gurdjieff relates it seems excessive. But it may not be.

The etymological roots of "Karapet," are interesting. *Kara* can mean "black" but also "joy" and *pet* can mean "heart" (as in parapet, a defensive construction on a fort or castle at the height of the heart (chest)). So this name might mean "black heart" or "joy of the heart." Neither meaning seems likely.

However, a little direct research into the name Karapet reveals the existence of the Saint Karapet Monastery, one of the oldest monasteries in "Greater Armenia," currently located in the Kurdish village of Chengeli in eastern Turkey. In Armenian, the monastery is named the Monastery of St. John Karapet, which is taken to mean the Monastery of St. John the Baptist. This possible meaning throws a different light on the tale of Karapet - and John the Baptist was indeed a precious jewel.

Steam whistle

A steam whistle is a device that produces sound using pressurized steam. Such whistles were used extensively on boilers, locomotives and ships. The mechanism is relatively simple and highly effective for long distance communication. The operator pulls a cord or lever, and a valve opens to release high-pressure steam from the boiler, which is forced through a narrow, circular opening. There is a resonator (usually a bell or hollow metal cyclinder), the sharp edge of which the steam jet hits, causing the steam bell to vibrate rapidly.

Karapet's steam whistle was intended to wake up all the railway workers, but it also woke up most of the other inhabitants of Tiflis.

The Tiflis local government

The Tiflis local government, as I recall it, even entered into a correspondence with the railway authorities ...

In the era to which Gurdjieff refers (around 1900), there are historical records from the Tiflis City Duma (the municipal government) and local newspapers of that period (such as Kavkaz or Iveria) which reflect tensions between the city and the Transcaucasian Railway.

The issue of the "daily steam whistle" was, in fact, a common point of urban friction across the Russian Empire. The main problem was, of course, noise pollution, which could in some places be amplified by surrounding hills. But also there was also the "daily" soot from the locomotives polluting the air and damaging the facades of buildings.

The Tiflis Railway Station was towards the center of the city—the city had grown rapidly around it. The Didube and Chugureti districts were heavily populated, and the constant shunting of engines and arrival/departure signals created a literal "noise corridor" through the heart of the city.

The railway whistle was more than just noise; it served as a de facto city clock. However, whistles might be blown at all hours of the night and early morning. To complicate the issue, The Transcaucasian Railway was a state-owned enterprise (under the Ministry of Ways of Communication), while the City Duma represented local interests. The local government frequently petitioned the railway administration to limit whistle-blowing within city limits (perhaps use bells instead) and relocate some of the "noisiest" maintenance shops away from the residential areas.

would, before taking hold of the rope and pulling it, wave his hand in all directions and solemnly, like a Mohammedan mullah from a minaret, loudly cry:

"Your mother is a—— , your father is a—— , your grandfather is more than a—— ; may your eyes, ears, nose, spleen, liver, corns ... " and so on; in short, he pronounced in various keys all the curses he knew, and not until he had done so would he pull the rope.

When I heard about this Karapet and of this practice of his, I visited him one evening after the day's work, with a small boordook of wine, and after performing this indispensable local solemn "toasting ritual," I asked him, of course in a suitable form and also according to the local complex of "amenities" established for mutual relationship, why he did this.

Having emptied his glass at a draught and having once sung the famous Georgian song, "Little did we tipple," inevitably sung when drinking, he leisurely began to answer as follows:

"As you drink wine not as people do today, that is to say, not merely for appearances but in fact honestly, then this already shows me that you do not wish to know about this practice of mine out of curiosity, like our engineers and technicians, but really owing to your desire for knowledge, and therefore I wish, and even consider it my duty, sincerely to confess to you the exact reason of these inner, so to say, 'scrupulous considerations' of mine, which led me to this, and which little by little instilled in me such a habit."

He then related the following:

"Formerly I used to work in this station at night cleaning the steam boilers, but when this steam whistle was brought here, the stationmaster, evidently considering my age and incapacity for the heavy work I was doing, ordered me to occupy myself only with releasing the steam into

Like a Mohammedan mullah

So when he would come in the morning to the rope with which he released the steam for the whistle, he would, before taking hold of the rope and pulling it, wave his hand in all directions and solemnly, like a Mohammedan mullah from a minaret, loudly cry:

That hauntingly beautiful chant you hear echoing from the minarets in Islamic countires is called the Adhan. It is a call to prayer, performed five times a day to notify the community that it is time for one of the obligatory prayers.

The person who recites the Adhan is called a Muezzin. The first person chosen for this role was Bilal ibn Rabah, a freed Abyssinian slave and close companion of the Prophet Muhammad. He was chosen specifically for his powerful and beautiful voice.

The Adhan translate to:

God is the Greatest (Allahu Akbar)

I bear witness that there is no god but God

I bear witness that Muhammad is the Messenger of God

Hasten to prayer

Hasten to success

God is the Greatest

There is no god but God

During the Fajr (dawn) prayer, the Muezzin adds a special line: "As-salatu khayrum minan-nawm," which means "Prayer is better than sleep."

While it is the specific job of the Muezzin to make the call to prayer rather than a Mullah who is generally a scholar or cleric, there is no religious rule forbidding a Mullah or Imam from doing it. In many small village mosques or private prayer rooms, there may not be a dedicated Muezzin. In these cases, the Mullah/Imam will often perform the Adhan himself. Also if the regular Muezzin is late or sick, the Mullah/ Imam will step in to ensure the call is made on time.

Boordock

> When I heard about this Karapet and of this practice of
> his, I visited him one evening after the day's work, with a
> small boordook of wine, and after performing this
> indispensable local solemn "toasting ritual," ...

It seems that the word Gurdjieff is using here is bardak
(Turkish) or bardaq (Arabic) or bardaqi (Georgian) or bardak
(Armenian). In each case it refers to a pitcher or drinking
vessel (possibly of clay or metal) used for pouring and storing
liquids.

Toasting ritual

In Georgia there are toasting rituals. At a traditional feast
called a Supra, it can be a highly structured, philosophical,
and poetic ceremony that can last for many hours. This is
maybe what Gurdjieff's "Toasting of the Idiots" derives from.

At a Supra the ritual is governed by a strict set of rules and a
specific hierarchy. The Tamada is the Toastmaster (or Master
of Ceremonies). No one may drink wine or make a toast
without his permission. He must be eloquent, witty, and have
a high tolerance for alcohol, as he guides the "emotional arc"
of the evening. He sets the theme for each round of drinking
and while he must drain his glass for every toast, he is
disgraced if he actually appears drunk.

If the Tamada wants someone else to elaborate on his toast,
he says "Alaverdi" to them. That person then continues the
theme with their own speech before the rest of the table
drinks. While the Tamada can improvise, a formal Supra
usually follows a specific thematic sequence. The first few
toasts are almost always:

- To God: Acknowledging the creator

- To the Motherland (Georgia): Specifically the phrase
  "Sakartvelos Gaumarjos!" (Victory to Georgia).

- To the Reason for Gathering: Whether it's a wedding,
  birthday, or a guest's visit.

- To the Deceased: A solemn moment to remember those no longer at the table.

- To New Life/Children: Following the toast to the dead to symbolize the cycle of life.

- Other common toasts honor peace, parents, women, and friendship.

There are specific rules of etiquette that need to be observed.

- Wine Only: Traditionally, toasts are made with wine or Chacha (strong grape brandy). Toasting with beer is considered an insult—historically, Georgians only toasted their enemies with beer, essentially wishing them bad luck.

- Listen in Silence: You must never talk or eat while the Tamada is speaking. It is a sign of deep respect.

- The "Bottoms Up" Rule: For some toasts, the Tamada will expect everyone to empty their glass. For others, a sip is fine, but you should always wait for him to finish speaking before raising your glass.

- Full Glasses: You should never toast with a half-empty glass. The designated wine-pourer will ensure your glass is constantly refilled.

The Supra is often described as a "secular prayer" because the toasts are meant to be sincere, emotional, and reflective.

Clearly Gurdjieff's meeting with Karapet did not have the status of a Supra, but Georgians rarely drink casually without some form of ceremony. If you are sitting down with just one other person for a few glasses of wine, there is no need for a Tamada, but the encounter will still follow a simplified, more intimate ritual.

In Georgia, drinking is almost never "automatic." Even between two friends, the act of drinking is always framed by a Sadghegrdzelo. Even with only two people, one person usually takes the lead as the host or the "designated" Tamada for that sitting. In such situations, Georgians often stick to a "holy trinity" of toasts that are considered the bare minimum for any meeting:

- To Our Meeting: Acknowledging the fact that you are together.
- To the Family: Specifically the parents or well-being of the other person's household.
- To Peace In Georgia: "Peace" is a deep-seated cultural wish, often used as the closing toast for a quick drink.

Amenities

This is an unusual choice of word. The local complex of "amenities" suggests that in this specific location, there is a complicated set of unwritten rules of social interaction. The "amenities" of conversation are things like small talk, offering a compliment, sharing a cup of tea, or apologizing for the intrusion before asking a difficult question. Such behaviors are established to ensure that neither person loses face or feels insulted.

Little did we tipple

The song title "Little did we tipple" is almost certainly incorrect. That is probably Orage's whimsical English translation of a song title that expressed the same sentiment, such as "We drank but a little." However, we have not been able to identify such a song.

In Georgian culture, drinking songs are a central part of the Supra. These songs are often polyphonic and complex. While there are many songs about wine and friendship, the sentiment—that the party has just begun and more wine is needed—is a very common theme in Georgian folk music.

Drinking honestly

"As you drink wine not as people do today, that is to say, not merely for appearances but in fact honestly, then this already shows me that you do not wish to know about this practice of mine out of curiosity, ...

These words from Karapet indicate to Gurdjieff that he has indeed achieved his aim of discovering the origin of Karapet's morning ritual.

the whistle, for which I had to arrive punctually every morning and evening.

"The first week of this new service, I once noticed that after performing this duty of mine, I felt for an hour or two vaguely ill at ease. But when this strange feeling, increasing day by day, ultimately became a definite instinctive uneasiness from which even my appetite for 'Makhokh' disappeared, I began from then on always to think and think in order to find out the cause of this. I thought about it all particularly intensely for some reason or other while going to and coming from my work, but however hard I tried I could make nothing whatsoever, even approximately, clear to myself.

"It thus continued for almost two years and, finally, when the calluses on my palms had become quite hard from the rope of the steam whistle, I quite accidentally and suddenly understood why I experienced this uneasiness.

"The shock for my correct understanding, as a result of which there was formed in me concerning this an unshakable conviction, was a certain exclamation I accidentally heard under the following, rather peculiar, circumstances.

"One morning when I had not had enough sleep, having spent the first half of the night at the christening of my neighbor's ninth daughter and the other half in reading a very interesting and rare book I had by chance obtained and which was entitled *Dreams and Witchcraft,* as I was hurrying on my way to release the steam, I suddenly saw at the corner a barber-surgeon I knew, belonging to the local government service, who beckoned me to stop.

"The duty of this barber-surgeon friend of mine consisted in going at a certain time through the town accompanied by an assistant with a specially constructed carriage and seizing all the stray dogs whose collars were without

An instinctive uneasiness

"The first week of this new service, I once noticed that after performing this duty of mine, I felt for an hour or two vaguely ill at ease. But when this strange feeling, increasing day by day, ultimately became a definite instinctive uneasiness ...

Karapet clearly senses the towns people's resentment of the the steam whistle. Whether there is a direct cause and effect is speculative. But there is likely to be an indirect effect. If you are aware that people are thinking negatively of you, it can have a tangible effect on your well-being.

It can trigger the body's "fight or flight" response, leading to increased cortisol levels. In other words, negative imagination has its impact.

Additionally, people who have negative thoughts about you may unconsciously show it through body language, tone of voice, or lack of eye contact. You might "sense" a bad vibe without knowing why. Also, some cultures and belief systems suggest that "the evil eye" or "negative energy" can affect a person directly. This may or may not be so.

'Makhokh'

ultimately became a definite instinctive uneasiness from which even my appetite for 'Makhokh' disappeared,

Makhokh (or Makhokhapur) is a traditional Armenian dish. It is a traditional soup associated with Lent. Its name comes from the Armenian word for "malt" or fermented grain. It is a sour soup made from fermented wheat (or barley), legumes (like chickpeas or beans), and dried fruits (like prunes or cornelian cherries).

It is a hearty, vegan-friendly dish designed to sustain people during fasting periods. In regions like Karin and Sassoun, there is a traditional "Dance of Makhokhapur" performed on the first day of Lent.

My neighbor's ninth daughter

"One morning when I had not had enough sleep, having spent the first half of the night at the christening of my neighbor's ninth daughter.

The most notable nine sisters are the children of Zeus and Mnemosyne (the goddess of memory and remembrance). Their daughters were the nine muses (in order by age): Calliope, Clio, Melpomene, Euterpe, Erato, Terpsichore, Urania, Thalia and Polyhymnia.

So perhaps Karapet was attending the birth of Polyhymnia (the one of many hymns) who is the patron of sacred poetry and hymns, as well as oratory, pantomime, geometry and meditation.

Dreams and Witchcraft

... and the other half in reading a very interesting and rare book I had by chance obtained and which was entitled Dreams and Witchcraft, ...

We can find no record of a book entitled *Dreams and Witchcraft*. Nevertheless, these are the two possibilities that that Karapet needs to investigate: whether his feeling of unease is caused by his own imagination (dreams) or whether by the psychic force of curses directed at him (witchcraft).

The barber-surgeon

... as I was hurrying on my way to release the steam, I suddenly saw at the corner a barber-surgeon I knew, belonging to the local government service, who beckoned me to stop.

In Tiflis, as elsewhere, the job of "dog-catcher" had a far lower status than the profession of "barber-surgeon." It was a menial "police adjacent" job.

At the turn of the 20th century, Tiflis—then part of the Russian Empire—faced significant issues with stray dogs and the constant threat of rabies. During the late 19th and early 20th centuries, many cities in the Russian Empire, including

Tiflis, implemented a municipal tax on dog ownership to control the stray population and fund sanitation efforts. The purpose of the tax was to ensure that only "responsible" citizens kept dogs, theoretically reducing the number of animals on the street.

When an owner paid the annual tax, they received a small metal tag (often called a "dog token" or *zheton*). This tag had to be attached to the dog's collar and served as a dog "passport." If a dog was found on the street without a visible tag, it was legally considered a stray.

Dog-catchers were often referred to as *zhivodyory* (which means "skinners") because they skinned the stray dogs for their hides. The "skinners" were usually paid per head, and made extra money from selling the hides. Dog pelts were used to make cheap furs, linings for winter boots, and caps. The dog-catchers also sold fat from the dogs to soap-boilers.

Wealthy residents could easily afford the tax and their dogs sported polished brass tags. For the poor, however, the tax was a burden. If a poor family's dog was caught without a tag, they usually couldn't afford the fine to "ransom" the dog back from the city pound, so the dog would inevitably be killed and processed by the skinners. The word *zhivoder* eventually became a general Russian insult for a cruel or bloodthirsty person, a meaning it still carries.

By the 1890s, the "barber-surgeon" as a singular hybrid profession was obsolete in Tiflis. The Russian Empire, which governed Georgia at the time, had a formalized medical system. Surgical tasks were performed by doctors or feldshers (trained medical assistants). Barbers were simply barbers.

So Gurdjieff's barber-surgeon is metaphorical. He would not have been a dog-catcher or a surgeon. Gurdjieff uses this metaphor several times throughout *The Tales* possibly to indicate a part of the psyche concerned with psychological health.

the metal plates distributed by the local authorities on payment of the tax and taking these dogs to the municipal slaughterhouse where they were kept for two weeks at municipal expense, feeding on the slaughterhouse offal; if, on the expiration of this period, the owners of the dogs had not claimed them and paid the established tax, then these dogs were, with a certain solemnity, driven down a certain passageway which led directly to a specially built oven.

"After a short time, from the other end of this famous salutary oven, there flowed, with a delightful gurgling sound, a definite quantity of pellucid and ideally clean fat to the profit of the fathers of our town for the manufacture of soap and also perhaps of something else, and, with a purling sound, no less delightful to the ear, there poured out also a fair quantity of very useful substance for fertilizing.

"This barber-surgeon friend of mine proceeded in the following simple and admirably skillful manner to catch the dogs.

"He somewhere obtained a large, old, and ordinary fishing net, which, during these peculiar excursions of his for the general human welfare through the slums of our town, he carried, arranged in a suitable manner on his strong shoulders, and when a dog without its 'passport' came within the sphere of his all-seeing and, for all the canine species, terrible eye, he without haste and with the softness of a panther, would steal up closely to it and seizing a favorable moment when the dog was interested and attracted by something it noticed, cast his net on it and quickly entangled it, and later, rolling up the carriage, he disentangled the dog in such a way that it found itself in the cage attached to the carriage.

"Just when my friend the barber-surgeon beckoned me to stop, he was aiming to throw his net, at the opportune

The municipal slaughterhouse

... taking these dogs to the municipal slaughterhouse where they were kept for two weeks at municipal expense ...

In Tiflis stray dogs were indeed taken to the municipal slaughterhouse. The slaughterhouse was the only facility equipped to handle the mass killing and industrial processing of animals. When the dog-catchers finished their rounds, the "dog-cart" was typically driven to the outskirts of the city where the municipal slaughterhouse was located. The Tiflis slaughterhouse had a dedicated section for "worthless" or "dangerous" animals.

Because it had drainage, hooks, and tools for skinning and boiling, it was the obvious place to process dog carcasses for their fat, bones and hides. The carcasses were boiled down to extract fat (for soap-makers). Bones were ground down for fertilizer. Pelts were sold to tanners.

The fishing net

"He somewhere obtained a large, old, and ordinary fishing net, which, during these peculiar excursions of his for the general human welfare through the slums of our town, he carried, ...

Tiflis dog-catchers usually patrolled the streets using heavy iron tongs or lassos to catch dogs and then throw them into their dog-cart. Gurdjieff's dog-catcher was unusual or even innovative in using a fishing net. The fishing net is also reminiscent of Christianity, and "fisher's of men."

moment, at his next victim, which at that moment was standing wagging his tail and looking at a bitch. My friend was just about to throw his net, when suddenly the bells of a neighboring church rang out, calling the people to early morning prayers. At such an unexpected ringing in the morning quiet, the dog took fright and springing aside flew off like a shot down the empty street at his full canine velocity.

"Then the barber-surgeon so infuriated by this that his hair, even beneath his armpits, stood on end, flung his net on the pavement and spitting over his left shoulder, loudly exclaimed:

"'Oh, Hell! What a time to ring!'

"As soon as the exclamation of the barber-surgeon reached my reflecting apparatus, there began to swarm in it various thoughts which ultimately led, in my view, to the correct understanding of just why there proceeded in me the aforesaid instinctive uneasiness.

"The first moment after I had understood this there even arose a feeling of being offended at myself that such a simple and clear thought had not entered my head before.

"I sensed with the whole of my being that my effect on the general life could produce no other result than that process which had all along proceeded in me.

"And indeed, everyone awakened by the noise I make with the steam whistle, which disturbs his sweet morning slumbers, must without doubt curse me 'by everything under the sun,' just me, the cause of this hellish row, and thanks to this, there must of course certainly flow towards my person from all directions, vibrations of all kinds of malice.

"On that significant morning, when, after performing my duties, I, in my customary mood of depression, was sitting in a neighboring 'Dukhan' and eating 'Hachi' with garlic,

The church bells

"Just when my friend the barber-surgeon beckoned me to stop, he was aiming to throw his net, at the opportune moment, at his next victim, which at that moment was standing wagging his tail and looking at a bitch. My friend was just about to throw his net, when suddenly the bells of a neighboring church rang out, calling the people to early morning prayers.

Clearly the church bell acts in a similar and anomalous manner to the steam whistle, distracting the dog from its preoccupation with a bitch, while calling people to early morning prayers.

Gurdjieff and dogs

We have provided enough background information to suggest that the story about Karapet and the dog catcher is clearly an allegory. This becomes clearer if we understand what the word "dog" symbolized to Gurdjieff. There is a wealth of material in the record of Gurdjieff's Paris meetings that explain this. Here are some extracts:

A: I am not able to be good to others.

GURDJIEFF: Perhaps you are not yet free?

A: I want to take advantage of everything, selfishly, for myself.

GURDJIEFF: You must work. Kill some 'dogs' in you. You only play your role in theory. At first you play it well, but very soon you forget and return to your ordinary state, to your nothingness. Your task will be to stay longer.

...

H B: At present, our dogs force us to use others to satisfy our desires.

GURDJIEFF: This is fertile ground for the development of being. Today you are an ordinary man; through working, try to be a real man. Later you will perhaps be a complete man, a real man. When you are aware of your dogs, struggle with them; this struggle is necessary in order for you to become a real man. This is fertile ground for work. And there are still more dogs in you that are invisible.[1]

And

GURDJIEFF: Everyone has a 'dog' inside him that plays the role of the devil. The secret for you is that whenever you do something, you expect a result, and you must not expect one. Perhaps you have an idea that has been crystallized in you. What you do now for the future is a guarantee for you. You should be pleased; the presence of this dog is a guarantee that you will have to work.

HT: I've tried to do these exercises sincerely as a service, but what arises in me when I persuade myself that I should not expect any result is this resignation I told you about, and which is another dog. I resign myself to doing the exercise without expecting results, but this is a bad attitude.

GURDJIEFF: Does this mean that you don't want anything, that you are not interested in anything? So, you have no aim? You haven't understood anything? If you've begun like this, you'll never get anywhere. You came here by accident. See Mme de Salzmann - she will explain things to you.[2]

And

MR. H.: Mr. Gurdjieff, sometimes self-remembering causes me boredom. I look forward to the end of my time for the exercise. There is something monstrous there, but I can't help it. Sometimes I feel wonderful fullness, but other times absolutely nothing. I can't help it, and when I have this condition, I don't know what it is.

MR. GURDJIEFF: This proves that in you the automatism is very strong, that there are in you many weaknesses, many dogs, many results to "desalt." We must kill them. How is it possible to be bored at a divine thing?

MR. H.: There's something missing in my self-remembering.

[1] *PARIS MEETINGS 1943, G.I.Gurdjieff, p43*
[2] *PARIS MEETINGS 1943, G.I.Gurdjieff, p72*

MR. GURDJIEFF: This is the symptom that there are a lot of dirty things inside you. You must clean all of that to become worthy of doing this exercise. Pay ten times more attention to cleaning your interior so that it becomes dignified. You are not.

There are too many dogs. Do you understand what I call dogs? The different things crystallized in you by life, by education. All of these results play the role of factors to create associations that always arise and drive you. These factors are numerous. We can't kill them completely. But we must make them functions. Today sometimes one, sometimes the other of these factors becomes your ego and directs you. The place of "Me"—as long as a true "Me" has not arrived—it is the head which must hold it, and play the role of the "Me."

MLLE. D.: Mr. Gurdjieff, when I remember myself, I never get a complete sense of satisfaction. The more I concentrate, the more I feel like I'm almost getting there. But something separates me. Afterwards I have rather an impulse of embarrassment and disgust.

MR. GURDJIEFF: Disgust with what?

MLLE. D.: Disgust with me, disgust..

(A silence)

MR. GURDJIEFF: Can you stay a while after the meeting? I'll tell you what bothers you.

MR. H. Mr. Gurdjieff, how to recognize these dogs, how to know which are the worst? And then, should we attack them? And how? Or do I just have to continue the general process?

MR. GURDJIEFF: In general, in everyone, these dogs are used to living around centers. This is their place. The factors are crystallized according to the preponderant centers. We have four centers, four localizations, four villages where these dogs live. In one village there are many, in another there are fewer, in yet another there are very few. Depending on the person, there are more or less dogs in each village.

These villages are Thought, Feeling, Sensation, and Sex— Sex which is even a very important village.

One person has more dogs in one village, another in another. It depends on which village is the most populated. My advice, in general, to kill these dogs, so that they no longer disturb you and so that they no longer have the strength to take the "I" in their hands, here it is - this advice is valid for everyone - we must first of all liquidate the dogs in the sex village. After, the others. We must first liquidate this intimate animal.

Afterwards, you will turn your attention to other villages. Knowing this rule, you will find out which village to continue through. But how to bind them? First you make it your task to never give these dogs the opportunity to function as before. Immediately, a blow to the head! Once you recognize your enemy, your first task is to struggle against him. Perhaps he is your real enemy. One after another you take all these dogs. And then you move on to another village. This is how you can gradually overcome your enemies.

I repeat, this is not about killing them. What is crystallized is forever. It can even become an asset if it is used as material, as a function. But dogs should never gain the upper hand, never should they have the possibility of fixing and taking the "I". This will be your task. And that goes for everyone here.

DR. H.: Mr. Gurdjieff, this sexual function, it is a function, it is not something that we must reduce and squash as much as possible?

MR. GURDJIEFF: We are not talking about functions, which are parts of us, but rather dogs, that is, weaknesses around our functions. The functions are the villages. We cannot change them. They are villages. But dogs, yes, we must change their breed.

DR. H.: What is the criterion for changing the breed? It varies with all...

MME. DE SALZMANN: Mr. Gurdjieff said it: it depends on the village. The functions are constituted differently in some and in the others.

P.L.: I think there are more dogs when the village is weak. Is this true?

MR. GURDJIEFF: The village is perhaps becoming weak because there are a lot of dogs to weaken it. Every dog has a name in these villages. I know all of their names.

(Mr. Gurdjieff jokes about the names of the dogs.)[1]

You may also wish to read or reread the story of Gurdjieff and Pogossian suddenly being surrounded by a pack of 15 Kurd sheepdogs and being unable to escape their attention.[2] As a counterpoint, there is also the story of Gurdjieff's loyal and exceedingly helpful dog Philos, who was also a Kurd sheepdog.[3]

The following are notes from a lecture given by Gurdjieff.

Lecture Thursday 10 November 1921

Dog. The Animal learns nothing. It participates, poses, argues, acts with—but with it is no progress.

Emotionality. The Animal is the emotionality.

It sits within and speaks and acts most of the day. You do not speak yourself.

It cries out, sobs, is terrified.

It leaps up, is overjoyed, wastes itself in enthusiasm.

It blinds the eyes. It never sees anything as it is.

It does not learn.

It does the same thing every day.

It remains the same in all situations.

It governs nearly all the behavior.

It is very difficult to see it. It conceals itself.

It seems to be in what we most value in ourselves.

It is turned to the world entirely.

[1] *PARIS MEETINGS 1944, G.I.Gurdjieff, p144-145*
[2] *Meetings With Remarkable Men, G.I.Gurdjieff, p94*
[3] *Meetings With Remarkable Men, G.I.Gurdjieff, p135-136*

It only understands in terms of the world.

It wishes to possess, to be praised. It uses everything for its own purpose. It does nothing except for self.

It is never free from fear.

Anything unusual is alarming to it. It seeks reassurance. It is behind much virtue.

Almost all virtue is emotional. The animal is emotionality. Emotionality is unconsciousness.

A knife is needed to cut through it: the knife of making conscious.

Otherwise there is no virtue. What is diffuse and unconscious contains no essence.

Virtue lies in essence. With the clear feelings is essence.[1]

So Gurdjieff's story of the dog-catcher can be taken as an allegory for the inner struggle necessary to work on oneself. The dogs are habitual mechanisms that live around our centers. Some—those that have a license—can be tamed to become useful functions, while others have to be destroyed. The destruction of these worthless dogs will be beneficial as their substance can be used productively for ourselves.

In respect of this Work, part of us that corresponds to a barber-surgeon (a healer of a kind) needs to undertake the task of managing these dogs. We note also the sexual dog (the one who was attracted by a bitch) dashes off when the church bell rings as a call to prayer.

My reflecting apparatus

"As soon as the exclamation of the barber-surgeon reached my reflecting apparatus, there began to swarm in it various thoughts which ultimately led, in my view, to the correct understanding of just why there proceeded in me the aforesaid instinctive uneasiness.

"The first moment after I had understood this there even arose a feeling of being offended at myself that such a simple and clear thought had not entered my head before.

---

[1] *Gurdjieff's Early Talks 1914-1931, G. I. Gurdjieff, p110*

"I sensed with the whole of my being that my effect on the general life could produce no other result than that process which had all along proceeded in me.

Because of this incident, Karapet realizes that his blowing of the steam whistle inevitably gave rise to negative vibrations being directed at him. He therefore began to consider how to neutralize their influence on him. His solution was to preemptively curse those who cursed him as described on p47 of *The Tales*.

"Your mother is a—— , your father is a—— , your grandfather is more than a—— ; may your eyes, ears, nose, spleen, liver, corns ... " and so on; in short, he pronounced in various keys all the curses he knew, and not until he had done so would he pull the rope.

Although Gurdjieff doesn't say so, it seems likely that he sees himself (and *The Tales*) in the role of Karapet, wakening us from our pleasant sleep, saving us from the barber-surgeon, and being cursed by us in return.

Dukhan

In the Caucasus (and also in Crimea) a dukhan (derived from the Persian/Arabic *dukkan*) refers to a small traditional tavern, shop, or restaurant.

Hachi with garlic

This is possibly what is called Khashi in Georgia and Khash in Armenia. It is a heavy, rich soup made by boiling cow or sheep's feet and stomach for many hours until the broth is thick and gelatinous. It is traditionally served unseasoned, but beside the soup bowl, a small dish of crushed garlic mixed with broth or water is provided. You stir in as much garlic as you desire to give the soup its flavor. It is eaten early in the morning (often as a hangover cure) with dried lavash bread and a shot of vodka.

I, continuing to ponder, came to the conclusion that if I should curse beforehand all those to whom my service for the benefit of certain among them might seem disturbing, then, according to the explanation of the book I had read the night before, however much all those, as they might be called, 'who lie in the sphere of idiocy,' that is, between sleep and drowsiness, might curse me, it would have—as explained in that same book—no effect on me at all.

"And in fact, since I began to do so, I no longer feel the said instinctive uneasiness."

Well, now, patient reader, I must really conclude this opening chapter. It has now only to be signed.

He who ...

Stop! Misunderstanding formation! With a signature there must be no joking, otherwise the same will be done to you as once before in one of the empires of Central Europe, when you were made to pay ten years' rent for a house you occupied only for three months, merely because you had set your hand to a paper undertaking to renew the contract for the house each year.

Of course after this and still other instances from life experience, I must in any case in respect of my own signature, be very, very careful.

Very well then.

He who in childhood was called "Tatakh"; in early youth "Darky"; later the "Black Greek"; in middle age, the "Tiger of Turkestan"; and now, not just anybody, but the genuine "Monsieur" or "Mister" Gurdjieff, or the nephew of "Prince Mukransky," or finally, simply a "Teacher of Dancing."

The sphere of idiocy

... if I should curse beforehand all those to whom my service for the benefit of certain among them might seem disturbing, then, according to the explanation of the book I had read the night before, however much all those, as they might be called, 'who lie in the sphere of idiocy,' that is, between sleep and drowsiness, might curse me, it would have—as explained in that same book—no effect on me at all.

The "sphere of idiocy" label that Gurdjieff uses may well be appropriate since in drowsiness there is rarely any clear thinking. Whether the solution adopted by Karapet has objective merit is difficult to ascertain. If Karapet believes he has shielded himself, that may be sufficient.

One of the empires of Central Europe

Gurdjieff spent roughly a year in Germany between August 1921 and late 1922 before eventually establishing his Institute near Paris, making several attempts to find a location for his institute. So he very likely rented a property there. However, he faced significant "obstruction" from the German government regarding residence permits and the official recognition of his Institute. So he chose France instead.

There is no reason to doubt Gurdjieff's story about signing a deceptive rental contract.

The signature

The chapter closes with Gurdjieff's very thorough signature. It has seven aspects:

- *He who in childhood was called "Tatakh"*: **Tat** in Armenian means "grandmother." So "Tatakh" may mean "notable grandmother." (Gurdjieff's grandmother was a well known healer and midwife.)

- *In early youth "Darky"*: This likely reflects Gurdjieff's swarthy complexion.

- *Later the "Black Greek"*: In *Life Is Real Only Then, When 'I Am'* Gurdjieff mentions some acquaintance calling him "Black Devil." In *Gurdjieff, A Master in Life*, Tcheslaw Tchekhovitch quotes someone referring to Gurdjieff as "you half-black Greek."

- *In middle age, the "Tiger of Turkestan"*: There is no record we can find of anyone referring to Gurdjieff by this nickname.

- *And now, not just anybody, but the genuine "Monsieur" or "Mister" Gurdjieff*: The name by which he was generally known once he began teaching.

- Or the nephew of *"Prince Mukransky"*[1]: There is no evidence that Gurdjieff was directly related to the Mukransky family. It is possible he was related by marriage in some way, but there is no known evidence.

- or finally, simply a *"Teacher of Dancing"*: Indeed.

Gurdjieff brackets this first chapter with an invocation to the Trinity (Law of Three) and this statement of his identity (Law of Seven).

---

[1] *The House of Mukhrani (often Russified as Mukhransky) is a princely branch of the Bagrationi dynasty, which ruled Georgia for over a millennium. While many family members held the title, Prince Mukhransky, there were only two in Gurdjieff's time: Prince Konstantin Bagration-Mukhransky (1889–1915) and Prince Alexander Bagration-Mukhransky (1853–1918). After the Red Army invaded Georgia in 1921, the family fled to Europe, primarily settling in Spain.*

Author's Biographical Notes

Robin Bloor was born in 1951 in Liverpool, UK. He obtained a BSc in Mathematics at Nottingham University and took up a career in the computer industry, initially writing software. From 1989 onwards, he became a technology analyst and consultant. He has thus been a writer of a kind ever since. In 2002 he was awarded an honorary Ph.D. in Computer Science by Wolverhampton University in the UK. He currently resides in and works from Austin, Texas in the USA.

In 1988, after drifting through several work groups, Bloor met and became a pupil of Rina Hands. Rina was a one-time associate of J. G. Bennett, a student of Peter Ouspensky's, and later, a pupil of George Gurdjieff. Following Gurdjieff's death, she remained part of J. G. Bennett's group for a while. Subsequently, she formed groups both in London, where she lived, and in Bradford in the North of England—initially in conjunction with Madame Nott. She was both an accomplished movements teacher and an inspirational group leader. She died in 1994 and is buried next to Jane Heap in a cemetery in North London.

Bloor leads a Group in Austin, Texas. Aside from the usual movements and Work activities, the group specializes in the study of Gurdjieff's writings and the study of Objective Science, as articulated by Ouspensky in *In Search of The Miraculous*, and by Gurdjieff in *The Tales*.

He has written a number of books about the Work. Details of some of these books are provided on the following pages.

Acknowledgements

The following individuals participated in study group meetings and thus made some contribution to the contenst of this book:

Robert Posen, Barbara Pennock, Michelle Fink, Ronald Jones, Rod Thorn, Paula Schmidt, Richard Miller, Sandra Whitmore, Lenny Schwartz, Sharon Johnson, John Amaral, Jean Armstrong, Jill Frank, John Heffel, Barbara Heffel, Ekant Billing, Gwynne Mayer, Jay & Judy Edwards, James Cummins, Stephen Frantz, Thomas Barnett, Vanya Nicole Klauss, Derek Sinko, Larry McMillan, Stephen Aronson, Sasa Jevtovic, Gary Reynolds, Frieda Billing, XJ Bao, Stewart Johnson, Roland Wiederaenders, Valerie Maddox, Jim Moats, Charles Alvis, James O'Donnell, Gloria Monda, Stephon, James Lowndes, Anne Little, Jeffrey Tripodi, Harry Gray, Kelly Connor, John Leidersdorff, DJ Scott, John Sleet, Eddie Purcell, Arthur Zuverza, Micah Newton, Laurie Barron, Bruce Stelmar, Dave Avery, Kristina Tatarinova, Meredith Finkelstein, Dirk Lehmann, Cindy Lee, Russell Turner, Ofelia Lopez, Sandra Lee, Petra Mandli, Jin Wang, Daphne Clement, Catalina Fuenzalida, Briji Waterfield, Bonnie Phillips, Carol Squire, Carole Orem, Adrian Fahy, Suzannah Silver, Bob King, Janet Mitchell, Ingrid Michel, Darren Woolsey, Paul McAtee, Joe Appel, Margaret Coit, Natalya Rafayelyan, Aaron Settles, Justin Speake, Barrington Nelson, Mark Geisser, Michael Liewald, Anthony Tan, Brigitte Dempsey, Patrick Carr, Mark Cruz, Amanda Dum, Wilfred Gonzalez and Jerome Sander. My apologies to anyone who attended any of the study meetings who is not included in this list.

For those who are interested, it is possible to join and participate in the current Tales Study group. To do so, register on this web page:

https://tofathomthegist.com/mem-tsg-sign-up-and-registration/

Or email: rbloor@littlecrowpress.com.

TO FATHOM THE GIST

Volume I: Approaches to the writings of G.I. Gurdjieff
Volume II: The Arch-Absurd
Volume III: The Arousing of Thought

These books provide a practical guide on how to approach Gurdjieff's masterpiece productively. The first analyzes and explains the different ways to think about the text and what it means. The second examines in detail how the book was written. This provides new and valuable insights Gurdjieff's writing activities and as a consequence provides new insights into the text.

The third book in this series compares the text of the two different versions of *The Tales* (*The 1931 Manuscript* and the 1950 published version). It focuses on the first 25 pages of the book, and also the text of *The Herald of Coming Good* providing a wealth of insight. These three books have become natural companions for readers of *The Tales*.

Other books from the Karnak Press

- Gurdjieff's Hydrogens Vol 1: The Ray of Creation by Robin Bloor
- Gurdjieff & Kundabuffer by Robin Bloor
- Readings, Prosaic and Poetic by Robin Bloor & Paula Schmidt
- Sayings From The Gurdjieff Work by Robin Bloor
- The 1931 Manuscript of Beelzebub's Tales by G. I. Gurdjieff
- The Revised Version of the 1931 Manuscript by G. I. Gurdjieff
- Beelzebub's Tales: Book One, Side by Side Comparison by G. I. Gurdjieff
- Beelzebub's Tales: Book Two, Side by Side Comparison by G. I. Gurdjieff
- The Herald of Coming Good [With Notes by R. Bloor] by G. I. Gurdjieff
- The Search For Meaning by Stephen Aronson
- As Inside, So Outside, As Above, So Below by Stephen Aronson
- Sacred Dances by Nella Liska
- Rodney Collin by Terje Tonne
- The Mirror of Light and Other Works by Rodney Collin